Kyle Idleman knows where we live and where we could live with God's help. His words are, at once, profound and practical. He is committed to helping us move in the right direction. If you need a helping hand in your journey, he'll point you to the right Person.

> Max Lucado, pastor of Oak Hills Church and bestselling author

Jesus never asked us to sit on the sidelines and cheer for his cause. In *Not a Fan*, Kyle Idleman will challenge you to grow from a fair-weather fan to a full-time follower of Christ.

> Craig Groeschel, senior pastor of LifeChurch.tv
> and author of *The Christian Atheist*

Get out your highlighter and let Kyle take you back to the core of Christianity. You may never enjoy being challenged more than by reading this clear, compelling, and winsome book!

> Lee Strobel, *New York Times* bestselling author

Not a Fan is truly a cutting edge message that will challenge even the most obedient Christians to re-look at their relationship with Christ. I highly recommend it to individuals and churches everywhere.

> Mike Huckabee, former governor of Arkansas
> and author of *Do the Right Thing*

The content in this book will rock your world.... and the author of this book is the real deal. Kyle is a great leader and follower—of Christ. His "not a fan" teaching was a defining moment and the start of a movement at our church.... it still continues today. *Not a Fan* can do the same in your life.

> Dave Stone, senior pastor at Southeast Christian Church

This book disrupts the status quo and challenges readers to follow Christ with greater devotion.

> Mark Batterson, lead pastor of National Community Church in Washington, DC

Kyle Idleman's *Not a Fan* is a crucial message for our time. It's a powerful call to commitment and to following Jesus with all our hearts that has challenged me in the best of ways!

> Jud Wilhite, senior pastor of Central Christian Church in Las Vegas and author of *Throw It Down*

Not a Fan is a book that every Christian should read and regularly re-read. I started to read the manuscript and could not stop until I finished. This is a NOW message for the Church, and my hope is that every believer who reads this will become an authentic follower of Christ.

> Christine Caine, founder of the A21 Campaign

Student edition

not a fan.

not a fan.

WHAT DOES IT MEAN TO
REALLY FOLLOW JESUS?

kyle idleman

ZONDERVAN®

ZONDERVAN.com/
AUTHORTRACKER
follow your favorite authors

ZONDERVAN

Not a Fan: Student Edition
Copyright © 2012 City on the Hill Studio, Inc.

This title is also available as a Zondervan ebook. Visit www.zondervan.com/ebooks.

Requests for information should be addressed to:

Zondervan, 5300 *Patterson Ave SE, Grand Rapids, Michigan* 49530

ISBN 978-0-310-74631-7 (softcover)

Cover design: *Curt Diepenhorst and Cindy Davis*
Cover photography: *Shutterstock®*
Interior design: *Beth Shagene*

Printed in the United States of America

13 14 15 16 17 18 /DCI/ 20 19 18 17 16 15 14 13 12 11 10 9 8 7 6 5 4 3 2 1

To my dad:
Following you taught me to follow Jesus.
I pray my kids will say the same.

contents

prologue

It's a Thursday afternoon, and I am sitting in the church sanctuary. It's empty now, but Easter is only a few days away. More than thirty thousand people will likely come to the weekend services, and I have no idea what I'm going to say to them. I can feel the pressure mounting as I sit there hoping that a sermon will come to mind. I look around at the empty seats hoping some inspiration will come. Instead there's just more perspiration. I wipe the sweat off my brow and look down. This sermon needs to be good. There are some people who only come to church on Christmas and Easter (we call them "Creasters"). I want to make sure they all come back. *What could I say to get their attention? How can I make my message more appealing? Is there something creative I could do that would be a big hit and get people talking?*

Still nothing. There is a Bible in the chair in front of me. I grab it. I can't think of a Scripture to turn to. I've spent my life studying this book and I can't think of one passage that will "wow" the Creasters. I consider using it the way I did as a kid. Perhaps you've done the same thing: Kind of like a Magic 8 Ball, you ask a question, open up the Bible and point on the page, and whatever it says answers your question.

Finally a thought crosses my mind: *I wonder what Jesus taught whenever he had the big crowds.* What I discovered would change me forever. Not just as a preacher, but as a follower of Christ. I found that when Jesus had a large crowd, he would most often preach a message that was likely to cause them to leave.

In that empty sanctuary I read of one such occasion in John chapter 6. Jesus is addressing a crowd that has likely grown to more than five thousand. Jesus has never been more popular. Word has spread about his miraculous healings and his inspirational teaching. This crowd of thousands has come to cheer him on.

After a full day of teaching, Jesus knows the people are getting hungry, and so he turns to his disciples and asks what all these people will do for food. One of the disciples, Philip, tells Jesus that even with eight months' wages, it wouldn't be enough money to buy bread for everyone to have a bite. From Philip's perspective, there really wasn't anything that could be done. But another disciple, Andrew, has been scanning the crowd and he tells Jesus of a boy who has fives loaves of bread and two small fish. Jesus takes the boy's sack lunch and with it he feeds the entire crowd. In fact, the Bible tells us that even after everyone had their fill, there was still plenty of food left over.

After dinner the crowd decides to camp out for the night so they can be with Jesus the next day. These are some big-time fans of Jesus. The next morning when the crowd wakes up and they're hungry again, they look around for Jesus, aka their meal ticket, but he's nowhere to be found. These fans are hoping for an encore performance. Eventually they realize that Jesus and his disciples have crossed over to the other side of the lake. By the time they catch up to Jesus, they're starving. They've missed their chance to order breakfast and they are ready to find out what's on the lunch menu. But Jesus has decided to shut down the "all you can eat" buffet. He's not handing out any more free samples. In verse 26 Jesus says to the crowd:

> I tell you the truth, you are looking for me, not because you saw miraculous signs but because you ate the loaves and had your fill.

Jesus knows that these people are not going to all the trouble and sacrifice because they are following him, but because they want some free food. Was it Jesus they wanted, or were they only interested in what he could do for them? In verse 35 Jesus offers himself, but the question is, *Would that be enough?*

> Then Jesus declared, "I am the bread of life. He who comes to me will never go hungry, and he who believes in me will never be thirsty."

Jesus says, *I am the bread of life.* Suddenly Jesus is the only thing on the menu. The crowd has to decide if he will satisfy or if they are hungry for something more. Here's what we read at the end of the chapter:

From this time many of his disciples turned back and no longer followed him (John 6:66).

Many of the fans turn to go home. I was struck by the fact that Jesus doesn't chase after them. He doesn't soften his message to make it more appealing. He doesn't send the disciples chasing after them with a creative handout inviting them to come back for a "build your own sundae" ice cream social. He seems okay with the fact that his popularity has plummeted.

As I sat in the sanctuary surrounded by thousands of empty seats, here's what became clear to me: it wasn't the size of the crowd Jesus cared about; it was their level of commitment.

I put the Bible back in the chair in front of me.

I cried.

God, I am sorry.

Almost as soon as I said it to him, I knew it needed to go further. A few days later on Easter Sunday, a crowd of thousands gathered and I began my sermon with a choked up apology. I told the crowd that I was wrong for being too concerned with what they would think and how many of them would come back. I think over the years my intentions were good; I wanted to make Jesus look as attractive as possible so that people would come to find eternal life in him. I was offering the people Jesus, but I was handing out a lot of free bread. In the process I cheapened the gospel.

Imagine it this way. Imagine that my oldest daughter turns twenty-five. She isn't married but she really wants to be.* I decide I'm going to help make that happen. So, imagine I take out an ad in the newspaper, put up a billboard sign, and make up T-shirts begging someone to choose her. I even offer some attractive gifts as incentives. Doesn't that cheapen who she is? Wouldn't that make it seem that whoever came to her would be doing her a favor? I would never do that. I would set the

---

* Note: all illustrations, literal or hypothetical, that make reference to any members of family are used without their expressed written permission.

standard high. I would do background checks and lie detector tests. There would be lengthy applications that must be filled out in triplicate. References would be checked and hidden cameras installed. If you want to have a relationship with her, you better be prepared to give her the best of everything you have. I don't want to just hear you say that you love her; I want to know that you are committed to her. I want to know that you would give your life for her.

Too often in my preaching I have tried to talk people into following Jesus. I wanted to make following him as appealing, comfortable, and convenient as possible. And I want to say that I am sorry. I know it's strange to start off a book with an apology, but I want you to know that the journey I'm inviting you on is one that I've been traveling. It's a journey I continue to be on, and I should tell you it hasn't been easy. It was more comfortable to be a part of the crowd.

I know typically you put something in the introduction that makes people want to read the book. You have a celebrity* write it, or you have someone else write it so that person can tell all the readers how great the writer is. At the very least the author should write something in the introduction of a book that makes people want to read it. I'm not sure if I've done that… probably not. My guess is an apology from a man who got it wrong for a long time doesn't exactly inspire confidence. But I just want to be clear that this book is not just information on a page or a pastor's commentary on the Scriptures. This book is written by one of those in the crowd in John 6 who thought Jesus was great but was really in it for the free meals.

I hope you will read this book and discover with me what it really means to follow Jesus. I will talk more about repentance than forgiveness, more about surrender than salvation, more about brokenness than happiness, and more about death than about life. The

---

* By "celebrity" I mean "Christian celebrities" like that guy who was the best friend of Charles on *Charles in Charge* and went on to become Bibleman, or the one guy who was on the *Dukes of Hazzard*—not the dark-haired one, the other one. You know, the guy who sometimes does commercials for Country Music compilation CDs. Oh, and if Blair off the *Facts of Life* couldn't do it, I also understand Tootie is a believer.

truth is, if you are looking for a book about following Jesus that lays out a comfortable and reassuring path, you won't find it here. Don't get me wrong, I want you to keep reading; I just want to be up-front and let you know there won't be a lot of free bread.

part 1

fan or follower?
an honest diagnosis

chapter 1

D.T.R.

Are you a follower of Jesus?

I would say the chances are pretty good that you just skipped over that question. You may have read it, but I doubt it carried much weight or had any real impact. But would you let me ask you this question again? It's the most important question you will ever answer.

Are you a follower of Jesus?

I know, I know. You've been asked this question before. Because it's so familiar there is a tendency to dismiss it. Not because it makes you uncomfortable. Not because it's especially convicting. The question is dismissed mostly because it feels redundant and unnecessary.

Chances are that if you are reading this book you fall into one of two groups:

1. The "I Like Jesus on Facebook" group. Your Facebook page says "Christian" and under activities you might even put "going to church." Under your "Likes," Jesus has made the cut. You are serious enough about your faith that you are happy to go to church with your parents or friends. In which case, when I ask you "Are you a follower of Jesus?" it seems rhetorical and you're ready to put the book down, or at least go back and look at the table of contents to see if there is a chapter that might be helpful. You recognize that this is an important question for many to consider, but asking you? Well, it's like sitting down with a group of junior high girls and asking how many of them know what "LOL" stands for. The answer to the question seems so obvious it doesn't seem worth answering. You've already dealt with it. Asked and answered. But before you move on too quickly, let me clarify what I am not asking. I am not asking the following:

Do you go to church?

Are your parents or grandparents Christians?

Did you raise your hand at the end of a message at church one time?

Did you repeat a prayer after a preacher?

Did you walk forward during a twelve-minute version of "How Great is our God"?

Do you own three or more Bibles?

Did you grow up going to VBS and/or church camp?

Is your ringtone a worship song?

When you pray are you able to utilize five or more synonyms for God?

I can keep going. Seriously, I can.

Have you ever worn a WWJD bracelet?

Do you have the Bible app on your iPod or phone?

Have you ever kissed dating good-bye?

Gals—Are your skirts more a dollar's bills length from your knee? Hold the bill horizontally; vertically doesn't count.

Guys—Is your hair cut above your collar?

Do you purposely say "Merry Christmas" instead of "Happy Holidays"?

When I ask "Are you a follower?" these are not the questions I'm asking. My point is that many of us are quick to say, "Yes, I'm a follower of Jesus," but I'm not sure we really understand what we are saying. To quote Inigo Montoya, "I do not think that means what you think it means."*

One of the most sobering passages of Scripture tells of a day when many who consider themselves to be followers of Jesus will be stunned to find out that he doesn't even recognize them. In the gospel

---

* If you recognized this quote as being from *The Princess Bride* then give yourself an extra point. It's a favorite movie among Christians (even though Kirk Cameron isn't in it). If you haven't seen this movie, I question whether or not you are truly being discipled by your parents.

of Matthew, chapter 7, Jesus tells of a day where everyone who has ever lived will stand before God. On that day many who call themselves Christians and identify themselves as followers will stand confidently in front of Jesus only to hear him say, "I never knew you. Away from me." If you've just assumed you are a follower of Jesus, I pray that this book would either confirm that confidence or it would convict you to reevaluate your relationship with Jesus and reaffirm your commitment to follow him.

2. The "Why does Facebook even ask about religion?" group.

If you are a part of this group, then you likely didn't buy this book. In fact, you would never spend your own money on it. But somebody who cares about you, and who might have Christian stuff all over their profile, gave it to you. Because it was a friend or a relative you figured you would at least read the first chapter to be polite. And maybe you skipped over the question "Are you a follower of Jesus?" It's not that you're against the question or offended by it. It just doesn't seem relevant to you. But it's irrelevant to you in a different way than the people in group number one. It's not that you have already answered the question; it's that the question doesn't seem worth answering. I get it, you mean no offense; you're just not into it.

It doesn't bother you that some people choose to follow Jesus. That's cool, but it's not your thing. Kind of like my friend who's so into *Star Trek* that he asks you things like "ta' SoH taH HoD?" (That's Klingon for "Do you think Spock should be captain?"*) And you don't really care. If that's what he likes, fine. But you don't get the appeal.

But ... what if? Would you pause for a moment and ask yourself, *What if all of life comes down to this one question? What if there really is a heaven and there really is a hell, and where I spend eternity comes down to this one question?* It may seem completely ridiculous, but if there is some part of you that considers this a minute possibility, then isn't it worth thinking through that question? As you read this book I hope you

---

* Please note that I did not personally translate this nor do I speak a word of "Klingon." I do, however, have a friend who speaks some Klingon. I ridicule and mock him, and I always do so in an actual language of real people.

would at least consider that this may be the most important question you ever answer. I believe that the reason we were put on this earth is to answer this one question. And the truth is, whether or not we do so consciously or intentionally, we all answer this question.

I want you to know up front that I'm not here to "sell" Jesus. I'm not going to try and talk you into following Jesus by presenting the parts that are most appealing. Because here's the thing, and don't tell the people in group #1 I said this, but many of them assume they are followers of Jesus, but the truth is they have never heard the unedited version of what Jesus taught about following him.

My guess is that after reading this book there will be people in group 1 and group 2 that turn down the invitation to follow Jesus. After all, when we read in the Gospels about Jesus inviting people to follow him, some people signed up, but most decided to walk away.

Time for the D.T.R.

So where do you start in determining if you really are a follower of Jesus? How do you decide if this is even something you would want to consider? Let's begin by having a D.T.R. talk with Jesus. Some of you will recognize what the letters D.T.R. stand for. If you're not sure, let me give you a hint. For a young man involved in a romantic relationship, these letters are often enough to strike fear into his heart. He likely dreads the D.T.R. talk. In fact, many young men will postpone, run away from, and put off the D.T.R. for as long as possible. I have even known a few guys who have terminated the relationship when they sensed that the D.T.R. talk was imminent.*

Now do you want to guess what D.T.R. stands for?

Define the Relationship.

This is the official talk that takes place at some point in a romantic relationship to determine the level of commitment. You want to see where things stand and find out if what you have is real.

---

* True Story: One of my friends faked hyperventilating to get out of the D.T.R. talk. By "one of my friends" I mean me.

In high school I went out on a first date with a girl that I really didn't know very well. We sat down in a booth at a restaurant and began the awkward first date conversation. During the appetizer I learned a little bit about her family. While we enjoyed the main course she told me about her favorite movie. And then it happened. While we were eating our dessert she asked me, and I quote: "Where do you see this relationship going?" On the very first date she was trying to have the D.T.R. talk. I got out of there P.D.Q.* That was the first and the last date.

I wasn't ready for that moment, but there comes a time when you need to define the relationship. It can be awkward. It can be uncomfortable. But eventually every healthy relationship reaches a point when the D.T.R. talk is needed. Is it casual or is it committed? Have things moved past infatuation and admiration and towards deeper devotion and dedication? You need to intentionally evaluate the state of the relationship and your level of commitment to the person.

So here's what I want to ask you to do. In your mind picture yourself walking into a local coffee shop. You grab a snack and get a drink and then walk towards the back where it isn't crowded and you find a seat at a small table. You take a sip of your drink and enjoy a few quiet minutes. Now, imagine that Jesus comes in and sits down next to you. You know it's him because of the blue sash. You're unsure what to say. In an awkward moment you try to break the silence by asking him to turn your drink into wine. He gives you the same look he used to give Peter. Before he has a chance to respond, you suddenly realize you haven't prayed for your food. You decide to say your prayer out loud, hoping that Jesus will be impressed. You start off okay, but understandably you get nervous and pray "Three things we pray: to love thee more dearly, to see thee more clearly, to follow thee more nearly, day, by day, by day." You quickly say "Amen" when you realize you're quoting Ben Stiller's prayer from *Meet the Parents*.

Before you have a chance to make things more awkward, Jesus skips past the small talk and gets right to the point. He looks you in the eye and says, "It's time we define this relationship." He wants to know

---

* If this isn't in your "text vocabulary," ask your parents what it means.

how you feel about him. Is your relationship with Jesus exclusive? Is it just a casual weekend thing or has it moved past that? How would your relationship with him be defined? What exactly is your level of commitment?

Whether you've called yourself a Christian since childhood, or all of this is new to you, Jesus would clearly define what kind of relationship he wants to have with you. He wouldn't sugarcoat it or dress it up. He would tell you exactly what it means to follow him. As you're sitting in that coffee shop listening to Jesus give you the unedited version of what kind of relationship he wants with you, I can't help but wonder if that question, "Are you a follower of Jesus?" would be a little more challenging to answer.

It may seem that there are many followers of Jesus, but if they were honestly to define the relationship they have with him I am not sure it would be accurate to describe them as followers. It seems to me that there is a more suitable word to describe them. They are not *followers* of Jesus. They are *fans* of Jesus.

Here is the most basic definition of fan in the dictionary:

"An enthusiastic admirer"

It's the guy who goes to the football game with no shirt and a painted chest. He sits in the stands and cheers for his team. He's got a signed jersey hanging on his wall at home and multiple bumper stickers on the back of his car. But he's never in the game. He never breaks a sweat or takes a hard hit in the open field. He knows all about the players and can rattle off their latest stats, but he doesn't know the players. He yells and cheers, but nothing is really required of him. There is no sacrifice he has to make. And the truth is, as excited as he seems, if the team he's cheering for starts to let him down and has a few off seasons, his passion will wane pretty quickly. After several losing seasons you can expect him to jump off the fan wagon and begin cheering for some other team. He is an enthusiastic admirer.

It's the woman who never misses the celebrity news shows. She always picks up the latest *People* magazine. She's a huge fan of some actress who is the latest Hollywood sensation. And this woman not only knows every movie this actress has been in, she knows what high school this actress went to. She knows the birthday of this actress, and she knows the name of her first boyfriend. She even knows what this actress's real hair color is, something the actress herself is no longer certain of. She knows everything there is to know. But she doesn't know the actress. She's a huge fan, but she's just a fan. She is an enthusiastic admirer.

And I think Jesus has a lot of fans these days. Fans who cheer for him when practice is rewarded with wins but who walk away when life is hard and they never seem to get the "W." Fans who sit safely in the stands cheering, but they know nothing of the sacrifice and pain of the field. Fans of Jesus who know all about him, but they don't know him.

But Jesus was never interested in having fans. When he defines what kind of relationship he wants, "Enthusiastic Admirer" isn't an option. My concern is that many of our churches in America have gone from being sanctuaries to becoming stadiums. And every week all the fans come to the stadium where they cheer for Jesus but have no interest in truly following him. The biggest threat to the church today is fans who call themselves Christians but aren't actually interested in following Christ. They want to be close enough to Jesus to get all the benefits, but not so close that it requires anything from them.

An Accurate Measurement

So Fan or Follower? The problem with asking that question of yourself is this: it's almost impossible to be straight-up honest. After all, if you say, "I'm a follower," what makes you so sure? What are the measurements that you use to define your relationship with Christ? What if we are measuring our relationship by breaking out a standard ruler, but he uses the metric system?*

Many fans mistakenly identify themselves as followers by using **cultural comparisons**. They look at the commitment level of

---

* Just being hypothetical. We all know Jesus doesn't use the metric system, that he uses Fahrenheit over Celsius, and he has thought the Dewey Decimal System was a bad idea from day one.

others around them and feel like their relationship with Jesus is solid. Essentially they grade their relationship with Jesus on the curve, and as long as they are more spiritual than the next guy, they figure everything is fine. That's why some fans are almost glad when it's found out that the Christian kid everyone admires actually watches porn or got caught smoking pot, and isn't as perfect as everyone thought. The curve just got set a little lower.

Have you noticed that when we compare ourselves to others as a way to measure our relationship with Christ we almost always put ourselves up against those who are on the JV team—spiritually speaking? When I was in high school, I had a tendency to take this approach in measuring myself as a son. I tried to convince my parents how good they had it by pointing to my friends who never honored their curfew or took out the garbage. When I gave my mom a birthday card I made sure she knew that I wasn't like my friend who forgot his mom's birthday. But here's what I've discovered: when I start comparing myself to others as a way to measure how I am doing as a son, I am doing so out of conviction and guilt that I'm falling short of who I know I should be as a son. And if you find yourself measuring your relationship with Jesus by comparing yourself to others, that is likely a self-indictment. It's a sign you know something isn't right. You are trying to justify yourself by comparing yourself to the person who's farther away from God than you.

Another measurement fans use is a religious ruler. They point to their observance of religious rules and rituals as evidence that they are really followers. After all, they reason, would a fan go to church every weekend, and put money in the offering, and volunteer in the nursery, and listen exclusively to Christian radio, and not see R-rated movies, and not even drink a wine cooler at the party? *Hello? Of course I'm a follower. I'm not doing all that for nothing!*

We have other ways to determine if we are followers. What about our family heritage? We think that because Mom and Dad are Christians, we're automatically in. Like the family membership at the neighborhood swimming pool: *as long as my parents are have paid the membership fee, I'm good to go.*

But here's the real question: how does Jesus define what it means to follow him? Because whatever measurement he gives is the one we should use.

Diagnosing Fandom

The Gospels record many examples of people having the D.T.R. talk with Jesus. In each encounter the person finds themselves in a position where the question "Fan or Follower?" has to be answered. Some are shown to be true followers while others are revealed to be nothing more than enthusiastic admirers. As we examine a number of these encounters, think of them as case studies that reveal different "symptoms" of being a fan.

If you have a sibling or two then you know that once they get sick it's only a matter of time before the entire house is contaminated. In my home we are constantly on medical websites trying to diagnose whatever ailment is being passed around. One of my favorite websites has a search function that allows you to enter in whatever symptoms you suffer from and then it gives the most-likely diagnosis. For example, if you type in "runny nose" and "nausea," the website informs you that it's likely the flu or a food allergy. If you add "lightheadedness," it narrows it down to a food allergy. If you take away "lightheadedness" and add "fever," then the diagnosis is more likely to be the H1N1 flu.* The more specific the symptoms, the more likely you are to get an accurate diagnosis.

The biblical accounts where Jesus requires people to define the relationship and honestly determine if they are true followers give us some telltale symptoms of being a fan. As we study these D.T.R. encounters with Jesus they will act as a mirror so we can have a more honest assessment of ourselves. Hopefully this will give us a more honest and accurate diagnosis of where we stand with Jesus. Fans often confuse their admiration for devotion. They mistake their

---

* I have a difficult neighbor and have wondered if he has some kind of contributing health issue. I entered in "adult acne," "irritability," "halitosis," and "excessive body hair," but no results could be found. If you know someone in the medical community, send them my way.

knowledge of Jesus for intimacy with Jesus. Fans assume their good intentions make up for their apathetic faith. Maybe you've already decided you're a follower and Not a Fan; well, I hope you keep reading, because one of the core symptoms of "fandom" is that fans almost always consider themselves to be followers.

So find a seat in the back of a coffee shop and read on. Let's honestly and biblically define the relationship. Are you a follower of Jesus? Or are you really just a fan?

a decision
or a commitment?

John 3 — Nicodemus

In John chapter 3 we read about a fan named Nicodemus. You should know that he wasn't just any fan. He was a well-known and well-respected man of God. Nicodemus was a member of the Sanhedrin, an elite group of community and religious leaders. He had been an admirer of Jesus for some time. Listening to the teaching of Jesus, he couldn't help but be inspired. He watched as Jesus worked incredible miracles, but it wasn't just his power that was impressive; it was his compassion and love.

Nicodemus was ready to take his relationship with Jesus to another level, but it wasn't that easy. It never is. There would be much to lose if he went public as a follower of Jesus. What would people think if they found out that Nicodemus was an admirer of this homeless carpenter-turned-rabbi? Why would he follow this hick from the sticks of Galilee? At the very least he would lose his position in the Sanhedrin and his reputation as a religious leader. Being a secret admirer of Jesus cost him nothing, but becoming a follower came with a high price tag. It always does.

So, Nicodemus finds himself at what would seem to be a surprising crossroads. He would have to choose between religion and a relationship with Jesus. This wouldn't be the last time that religion would get in the way of someone following Jesus. There is no way to truly become a follower of Jesus without losing your religion.

In John chapter 3 we read about his D.T.R. moment with Jesus. The story begins with the time of day it was when Nicodemus approached Jesus:

> He came to Jesus at night ... (v. 2).

It would be easy to overlook this detail and dismiss it as insignificant. But ask yourself, *Why would he come to Jesus at night?* He had plenty of opportunities during the day. Jesus was teaching in public places where it would have been quite convenient for Nicodemus to talk to him for a few minutes. In fact, given his position as a religious leader, the other people would have quickly stepped out of the way for Nicodemus to have the time and attention of Jesus. But Scripture says, "He came to Jesus at night ..."

At night no one would see him. At night he would avoid awkward questions from the other religious leaders. At night he could spend time with Jesus without anyone knowing. If he could speak with Jesus at night when no one was around, maybe he could begin a relationship with Jesus without having to make any real changes. He could follow Jesus without it impacting his job. In fact, his friends and family wouldn't even have to know. He could talk to Jesus at night and quietly make a decision in his heart to believe in Jesus; that way it wouldn't disrupt his comfortable and established life. That sounds like a lot of fans I know. Fans are happy to follow Jesus as long as that doesn't require any significant changes or have negative implications.

Here is the reality that Nicodemus is about ready to have impressed on him: There is no way to follow Jesus without him interfering with your life. Following Jesus will cost you something. For Nicodemus it would cost him a powerful position. It would cost him the respect of his co-workers. It would cost him his source of income and livelihood. It would cost him friendships. It would likely cost him some family relationships. It would cost him some future dreams, and certainly some popularity. This brings up a very telling question for most fans: has following Jesus cost you anything? I don't mean for that to be a rhetorical question. Take a moment and jot down what following Jesus has cost you. How has following Jesus interfered with your life? Or maybe you write down some ways you can see that following Jesus might cost you something in the future.

Most of us don't mind Jesus making some minor change in our lives, but Jesus wants to turn our lives upside down. Fans don't mind him doing a little touch-up work, but Jesus wants complete renovation. Fans come to Jesus thinking tune-up, but Jesus is thinking overhaul. Fans think a little makeup is fine, but Jesus is thinking makeover. Fans think a little decorating is required, but Jesus wants a complete remodel. Fans want Jesus to inspire them, but Jesus wants to interfere with their lives.

Nicodemus begins his conversation with Jesus by making it clear that he has decided that Jesus really is from God. He had come to a point of belief, but where would he go from there? Jesus doesn't waste time but gets right to the heart of why Nicodemus is coming to him at night instead of in the openness of the day. He tells Nicodemus in verse 3 that he must be born again. That would have been hard for this religious leader to hear. He had memorized the first five books of the Bible when he was a boy and had spent his adult life building a religious resume. But Jesus makes it clear to Nicodemus that his righteous acts and religious rituals are not the measurements he is using. Nicodemus must humble himself and be born again into a whole new way of life.

Nicodemus had made a decision about Jesus, but that's not the same as following him. Jesus would not accept a relationship with Nicodemus where he simply believed; Jesus wanted Nicodemus to follow. Jesus didn't just want Nicodemus just at night; he wanted Nicodemus during the day too.

Diagnosing Fandom —
QUESTION 1: Have You Made a Decision for Jesus or Have You Committed to Jesus?

There is a difference. There shouldn't be. But there is a difference. Many have made a decision to believe in Jesus without making a commitment to follow Jesus. The gospel allows for no such distinction. Biblical belief is more than just accepting something as fact in your mind or saying the right things. Many fans have repeated a prayer or raised their hand or walked forward at the end of a sermon and made a decision to believe, but there was never a commitment to follow. Jesus never offered such an option. He is looking for more than words of belief; he's looking to see how those words are lived out in your life. When we decide to believe in Jesus without making a commitment to follow him, we become nothing more than fans.

Imagine going to a wedding and watching a groom on his wedding day look at his beautiful bride, and with a tear in his eye he speaks words of devotion "... forsaking all others until we are parted by death." You're moved by his words and the decision he has made. But imagine if the next week you find out that while the newlyweds were away on their honeymoon the groom was unfaithful to his bride. Suddenly those words would hold no value. They would be worthless. Let's also imagine that you find out he never even intended to be faithful and had told his best man as much just before the wedding. You would conclude that those words he emotionally expressed and publicly declared meant little because they were not validated by faithful commitment.

We tend to define belief as the acceptance of something as real or true. But biblical belief is more than just an intellectual acceptance or a heartfelt acknowledgment; it is a commitment to follow. Following by definition requires more than a decision you make in your head while sitting in a pew; following calls for movement. One of the reasons our churches can become fan factories is that we have separated the message of "believe" from the message of "follow." After separating the two messages, they get out of balance.

If you read through the four Gospels that tell of Christ's life, you'll find that Jesus says "Believe in me" about five times. But care to guess how many times Jesus said "Follow me"? About twenty times. Now I'm not saying that following is more important than believing. What I am saying is that the two are firmly connected. They are the heart and lungs of faith. One can't live without the other. If you try and separate the message of follow from the message of believe, belief dies in the process. Our churches will continue to be full of fans until we bring together these words that should never have been separated to begin with. Following is part of believing. To truly believe is to follow.

Most fans I have talked with have been in church or in Christian communities where their belief in Jesus was constantly being emphasized and strengthened, but what it actually meant to follow Jesus was never made very clear.

For those of you who work out at a gym several times a week, you've probably noticed that there are a few "gym rats" who always seem to be there. At my gym you can typically spot them walking aimlessly around the weight room and staring at themselves in the mirror. But I've noticed something about these guys. They tend to have huge upper bodies and teeny tiny legs. They spend hours working on their chest, biceps, and triceps, but the calves and the thighs don't get much attention. As a result they are completely out of balance.*

This is what we have often done with our approach to discipleship. In teaching people what it means to be a Christian, we spend much of our time and effort bringing them to a point of belief without clearly calling them to follow. We have taken "believe" and we have written that in capital letters with bold print: **BELIEVE.** But everything that has to do with following has been put in small print: follow.

Maybe that's your story. When you heard the gospel, someone talked at great length and with passion about you making a decision to believe, but said little about the fact that this commitment would necessarily change the way you live. I call this "selling Jesus."

---

* This description is for illustrative purposes only. Any persons from my gym matching this description need to know this is purely coincidental and should not be taken personally.

Selling Jesus

Have you ever been walking through the mall, minding your own business, only to be assaulted by one of the sales people at the merchandise booths that are set up in the middle of the hall? They know they only have a brief moment to get your attention so they start talking about how fantastic their product is. But in their sales pitch, notice what they don't mention. They don't mention price. They say nothing of what it will cost you. If it's a cell phone, they don't mention what kind of contract you'll have to sign or what kind of commitment you'll be making. They only focus on the positives. They say what you want to hear. Then, after you've made a decision, they'll quickly skip the fine print. They just want to make a sale.

Sometimes when we talk about Christianity we can be reluctant to shine a bright light on the cost and the commitment in fear that we might not make the sale.

Jesus doesn't hold back with Nicodemus. Following Jesus would require a commitment that would cost Nicodemus a great deal. As we look at what it means to follow Jesus, this will become a theme. In fact, it's true throughout all of Scripture. Moses couldn't follow God without standing in front of Pharaoh. Noah couldn't follow God without building an ark that would bring ridicule from his neighbors. Daniel couldn't follow God by praying to him alone without being thrown into a lions' den. Following Jesus isn't something you can do at night where no one notices. It's a twenty-four-hour-a-day commitment that will interfere with your life. That's not the small print—that's a guarantee.

Have you ever been flipping through the channels late at night and come across the ShamWow guy? If you haven't seen this guy, google "shamwow commercial." But don't do it unless you're prepared to actually buy a ShamWow. The ShamWow is a glorified towel. But when you hear him tell about it you'll be ready to sign over your allowance for the next year. Or maybe you've seen other infomercials telling you how to get a scholarship or government grant. There are numerous infomercials that tell you how to get rich quick. An obnoxious spokesperson is looking into the camera and asking questions like,

Would you like to make more money? Would you like to own a second home in Fiji? Would you like to drop out of school and never worry about money again? And then you're asked, *Does that sound like something you might be interested in?* Then the salesperson goes on to explain that all this can be yours for free. You don't even have to pay shipping and handling.

How do you respond to that? How can you say no? It costs you nothing and offers you everything. And I wonder if some well-intentioned preachers may have missed their calling as late-night infomercial salesmen. Because many people heard a gospel presentation that went something like this: *How would you like to live forever? Would you like to have your sins forgiven and have a fresh start? Do you want to spend eternity in paradise instead of burning hell?* Some take it even further ... *Would you like to live a prosperous life? Are you ready to claim the health and wealth God has in store for you? Does that sound like something you might be interested in?* It's what I call a "ShamWow Sermon." And while some people rolled their eyes and changed the channel, a lot of fans signed up.

They ordered a gospel that cost them nothing and offered them everything. While salvation in heaven is a free gift from God that comes through putting our trust in Christ, you will find that in this world putting your trust in Christ will cost you.

So in case someone left it out or forgot to mention it when they explained what it meant to be a Christian, let me be clear: There is no forgiveness without repentance. There is no salvation without surrender. There is no life without death. There is no believing without committing.

At the church where I am a pastor, someone sent an email asking to be removed from the church membership. The stated reason for leaving read as follows:

I don't like Kyle's sermons.

That's all it said. That begs for some kind of explanation, so I decided to call the person. I checked the name of the person and got the phone number. I wanted to confirm that it wasn't my mom. That would have been awkward. I was driving in my car and called him on my cell phone. I would suggest that when making this type of call from your personal phone, first go to "Settings" on your phone, then "Show my caller ID," and then turn to "Off." Do not attempt while driving. When he answered I simply said, "Hey, this is Kyle Idleman. I understand you're leaving the church because you don't like my sermons."

There was a brief silence. I caught him off guard just as I had planned. It was awkward for a moment, and then he started talking—rambling really—trying to express what he meant. Somewhere in the middle of his lengthy explanation he said something. What he said was not meant to be encouraging, but his words caused me to breathe such a sigh of relief that tears came to my eyes. I pulled over to the side of the road, grabbed a pen, and wrote down what he said:

Well ... whenever I listen to one of the messages I feel like you are trying to interfere with my life.

Yeah, umm, that's kind of like my job description. But do you hear what he was saying? He's saying—*I believe in Jesus, I'm a big fan, but don't ask me to follow. I don't mind coming to church on the weekends. I'll pray before meals. I'll do a bit of recycling. I'll even slap a Jesus fish on my bumper. But I don't want Jesus to interfere with my life.* When Jesus defines the relationship he wants with us he makes it clear that being a fan who believes without making any real commitment to follow isn't an option.

When Nicodemus meets with Jesus in John 3 we're left wondering what he's going to do. The silence seemed to identify him as a fan who wasn't even an enthusiastic admirer, but a secret admirer who never managed the courage to take his relationship with Jesus from words of belief to a life of commitment.

But it turns out this isn't the last we read of Nicodemus. The next time we meet up with him is in John 7. The popularity of Jesus has grown immensely. The religious leaders are overcome with jealousy and fear. We read that the Sanhedrin meet together to find a reason to silence Jesus. Part of their role as the religious leaders was to judge false prophets. They needed to drum up some kind of accusation or charge that would indict Jesus as a false teacher. Nicodemus is sitting among his peers as they conspire to bring Jesus down. He is just one of seventy-two religious leaders that were part of this ruling body. Nicodemus believes Jesus is from God, but would he say anything? Would his belief translate into any kind of commitment? I'm sure he sat there hoping someone else would say something in defense of Jesus. Surely he wasn't the only one who believed. His mind is racing with what it's going to cost him if he goes public with his conviction. Then we read in verse 51 that Nicodemus comes to the defense of Jesus:

John 7:51: *"Does our law condemn anyone without first hearing him to find out what he is doing?"*

Though he stops short of saying what he believes, he does risk his career and reputation and publicly speaks up on behalf of Jesus. This is no longer a private conversation about what he believes. He allows what he believes to interfere with his work, his relationships, and his financial future. In that moment he stops being just a fan, and begins the journey of following.

When he speaks out in defense of Jesus, we read in verse 52 that the rest of the Sanhedrin responded this way:

"Are you from Galilee, too?"

I know that doesn't seem very harsh, but they are clearly trying to embarrass Nicodemus for associating with Jesus. Galilee was a small insignificant region that no one was proud to be from. Apparently they even had a saying in those days, "Can anything good come out of Galilee?"* The Sanhedrin laughed at Jesus because of where he was from, and now they use it to attack Nicodemus. It was meant to be a hard shot to his ego and a threat to his religious reputation that he had worked so hard to establish. It was a reality check for Nicodemus.

I've discovered there is almost always a moment like this for believers. They are put in a position where they have to decide between being a fan or a follower.

---

* Similar to our saying in Kentucky, "Can anything good come from Duke?"

Any hope Nicodemus had that he could follow Jesus without it interfering with his life was shot down with that one question, *"Are you from Galilee, too?"*

At the end of John's gospel, there is one other brief reference to Nicodemus. In John chapter 19 Jesus has been crucified and his body is being prepared for burial. And then we read that Nicodemus brought "a mixture of myrrh and aloes, about 75 pounds." This would have been an extremely expensive and costly gesture. And make no mistake; this gesture cost him more than just money. There was no longer any chance of hiding his affection.

In fact, when most others had abandoned Jesus, or were hiding in fear, Nicodemus makes this great gesture of affection and devotion. Things had moved past words of belief expressed in the darkness of night. He was no longer a secret admirer. He wasn't just an enthusiastic admirer. It seems he had become a follower. That's the last time we read of Nicodemus in Scripture. Christian tradition asserts that he was martyred sometime in the first century.

If you have believed in darkness, Jesus now invites you to follow him in the light.

not a fan story

Shelbi Draper

I have been going to doctor after doctor since I was about seven years old, complaining of pain in my legs. Until I was in middle school, the doctors always dismissed it as "growing pains." Then when I was sixteen, with hopes of a driver's license and a first kiss, my life changed. My trip to this doctor's office was different. I would receive news that I was being prepared for spiritually, but undone by emotionally. After a regular physical examination the doctor said these unforgettable words that would change my life forever: "Shelbi, you can get up off the floor on your own today, but within three years you won't be able to get up by yourself ever again." In the midst of shock, my first feeling after hearing those words was, surprisingly, an overwhelming peace. In that moment, I rested in knowing that God has a plan for me. My mother and I walked out that day, and just sat in the car. I can still remember the sound of her weeping in disbelief. Every tear I cry over the excruciating pain I feel, from just trying to keep up with the pace of every other teenager, I now surrender to the promise of a new day when I will be victorious over muscular dystrophy. My doctor may be right in saying that in the future I may not be able to pick myself up on my own. However, I kind of feel like that's the way it's meant to be for everyone — we aren't supposed to be able to pick ourselves up. He not only picks me up, he carries me, because truly, "Apart from him I can do nothing." Through this pain, my faith has become real to me in a different way. I am learning what it means to be completely dependent upon my Savior. I cannot and will not follow Jesus in the dark. I won't hide behind my weakness and disease. I will follow him in the light and I will live in hope and faith. Jesus alone gives me grace each new morning with the rising of the sun. In an ironic way, muscular dystrophy has saved me. It has saved me from being just a fan of Jesus. I now long to follow him so closely that he can snatch me up the second I start to hit the floor. My name is Shelbi Draper, and I am not a fan.

knowledge about him or intimacy with him?

Luke 7

When I was preaching in Southern California there was a soap opera star for the daytime show *General Hospital** who went to our church. His name was Réal Andrews. He was coming to church every weekend and really growing as a Christian. One day he approached me about coming to an upcoming *General Hospital* "fan day." He explained that he wanted to have a Gospel Hour for his fans. Even though I'm not really into soap operas and I tend to avoid gatherings that would be called "Gospel Hour," I said he could count me in.

For the *General Hospital* fan day, he rented out this big ballroom at a Hollywood hotel, and he had me preach to these fans of the soap opera from all around the country. It was very surreal, to say the least. I walked in and there were hundreds of fans of Réal. To me, he was just my friend at church. But to these fans, he was an incredible star on a legendary soap opera. When I came in they were playing a trivia game in which fans competed to show who knew the most about Réal Andrews. And they knew everything about him. They certainly knew a lot more than I knew. They knew where he was born, which high school he went to, the ages of his kids—even his food allergies. So I'm sitting there, a little amazed and a little weirded out by the whole thing. I was struck by the fact that all these fans seemed to know him better than I did.

But if you think about it, that's not really accurate. Those fans didn't really *know* Réal. They just knew about him. They knew the facts and

---

* For those who care, he was Detective Marcus Taggert.

the trivia, but I knew what his journey to Christ was like. They knew how many episodes he'd been in and they could tell you about the various struggles his character had been through on the show, but I knew what his character was like off-camera. I knew Réal as a real person and was friends with him. The fans just knew about Réal.

In the Bible, we read about a group of religious leaders known as the Pharisees. The Pharisees knew a lot about God. When someone wanted to play "Bible Trivial Pursuit,"* "God-opoly," or "Bible Baseball," they would dominate. They knew about God, but what we discover is they really didn't *know* him.

In Matthew 15:8 Jesus describes the Pharisees this way:

> These people honor me with their lips, but their hearts are far from me.

That description seems to fit most fans I know. Like the Pharisees, many fans have given their minds to the study of God, but they never surrendered their hearts. These were men who had plenty of knowledge about God, but they didn't really know God. What separates fans from followers is often the difference between knowledge and intimacy.

In Luke 7, Jesus has been invited over for dinner by one of these Pharisees. His name was Simon. Most likely Simon extended the invitation after Jesus finished teaching. Apparently, this was before the days of having a potluck meal after the sermon.† For Simon, having the visiting rabbi over for a meal would have been considered a religious merit, like when you sit down to eat with your friends and you bow your head and say a silent prayer. You may not actually be praying—you may just be counting to ten. But it's what you are supposed to do and so you do it. That's Simon's spirit here. Jesus should have been

---

* Q: Old Testament prophet who was the son of Amoz? A: Who is Isaiah? I'll never forget this one because it cost me the sixth grade championship. It was worth 100 Bible bucks.
† If you didn't grow up in a real church, a "potluck" meal is traditionally offered in the Fellowship Hall of the church. Everyone brings a dish that is set out on a table for all to enjoy. A popular item at potlucks is the Jell-O salad, which consists of leftovers such as beets, tuna fish, Spam, Velveeta cheese, and peanut butter mixed together with Jell-O. Typically it's made by someone named Wilma or Betty.

considered the guest of honor for this meal, but it quickly becomes apparent that Simon was spending time with Jesus out of a sense of duty instead of a desire to honor him.

There were certain rules of etiquette at a dinner like this. For instance, the customary greeting for an honored guest would have been a kiss. If the guest was a person of equal social rank, then the host would greet the guest with a kiss on the cheek. If it was a person of especially high honor, the host would greet the guest with a kiss on the hand. To neglect the kiss of greeting was the equivalent to openly ignoring somebody. It would be like having a person come into your home and refusing to even acknowledge their presence in some way. Not saying hi, not shaking their hand, not even giving them the head nod while simultaneously raising the eyebrows, nothing.

Another part of first-century Middle East etiquette involved the washing of feet. The washing of feet was mandatory before meals. If you truly wanted to honor the guest then you would do it yourself. If not, you might have your servant wash the feet of your honored guest. At the very least you would simply give the water to your guest to wash his or her own feet.

For an especially distinguished guest, you might also give them some olive oil for anointing their head. This was inexpensive oil, but it was still considered an especially hospitable gesture. But when Jesus comes to the house of Simon, there is no kiss of greeting. There is no washing of feet. There is no oil for his head. And these were not accidental oversights. This was quite deliberate. Jesus was ignored and insulted.

Don't miss the irony of this moment. Simon has spent his life studying the Scriptures. By the time he was twelve he had the first twelve books of the Bible memorized. By the time he was fifteen he had memorized the entire Old Testament. He had committed to memory the more than three hundred prophecies about the coming Messiah. Yet he doesn't realize it is the Messiah who now sits at his table with a hand that hasn't been kissed, feet that haven't been washed, and a head that hasn't been anointed. He knew all about Jesus, but he didn't know Jesus.

Diagnosing Fandom —
QUESTION 2: Do You Just Know about Jesus, or Do You Really Know Him?

Fans have a tendency to confuse their knowledge for intimacy. They don't recognize the difference between knowing about Jesus and truly knowing Jesus. In church we've often got this confused. We have established systems of learning that result in knowledge, but not necessarily intimacy.

Think about it: We love having Bible *studies*, many of which include some kind of *workbook*. We go through a Bible *curriculum* that often has *homework*. Messages are often accompanied by a *handout* that allows you to fill in the blanks and take notes. Many preachers refer to their sermons as a *lesson* or a *lecture*. If you grew up in the church, then you probably went to Sunday *school*, where you had a *teacher*. In the summer you may have gone to vacation Bible *school*. Maybe you even competed in Bible Bowl competitions, all of which are won or lost depending on how much biblical *knowledge* you've accumulated and how fast you can raise your hand or hit a button.

Now don't get me wrong, studying and learning from God's Word is invaluable. Jesus referenced, read, and quoted all kinds of passages from the Old Testament, ample proof that he had studied God's Word with great care and diligence. The problem isn't knowledge. The problem is that you can have knowledge without having intimacy. In fact, knowledge can be a false indicator of intimacy. Clearly where there is intimacy there should be a growing knowledge, but too often there is knowledge without a growing intimacy. Some of you have seen this with your mom and dad. You can tell they have a close intimate relationship because of how much they know about each other. Your mom says, "You can ask your dad, but I know what he's going to say." Or you go out to eat and your mom is in the restroom but your dad goes ahead and orders for her. Knowledge is part of intimacy, but just because there is knowledge doesn't mean there is intimacy. You can know a lot about a person, but that doesn't necessarily mean you are close.

Like this Pharisee in Luke 7, and like many fans today, I spent a number of years confusing my knowledge about Jesus for intimacy with Jesus. For example, for as long as I can remember, I've had the books of the Bible memorized in order—all sixty-six of them. Not only that, I can actually say the books of the Bible in one breath. Don't try to act like you're not impressed. So here's the book version of my recitation of the books of the Bible. I know it's not quite the same, but if you hold your breath and read them out loud without taking a breath, you might get a sense of what a spiritual accomplishment this really is.

Take a deep breath. Here we go:

Genesis, Exodus, Leviticus, Numbers, Deuteronomy, Joshua, Judges, Ruth, 1 and 2 Samuel, 1 and 2 Kings, 1 and 2 Chronicles, Ezra, Nehemiah, Esther, Job, Psalms, Proverbs, Ecclesiastes, Song of Solomon, Isaiah, Jeremiah, Lamentations, Ezekiel, Daniel, Hosea, Joel, Amos, Obadiah, Jonah, Micah, Nahum, Habakkuk, Zephaniah, Haggai, Zechariah, Malachi, Matthew, Mark, Luke, John, Acts, Romans, 1 and 2 Corinthians, Galatians, Ephesians, Philippians, Colossians, 1 and 2 Thessalonians, 1 and 2 Timothy, Titus, Philemon, Hebrews, James, 1 and 2 Peter, 1, 2, and 3 John, Jude, and Revelation.

Did you make it? The truth is that Jesus doesn't care that I can do that. He's not impressed with my knowledge or my talent. Admittedly, I kind of wish he was. I think it would be great if that's what it came down to on Judgment Day. Jesus gets all of us together and he says, *Okay, here is how it's gonna go. All of you who can say the books of the Bible in one breath, just step over on this side. And if you can't do that—I'll give you two tries— just go on down the steps there. And when you think you've gone too far, keep going.* I'm pretty certain that's not how it's going to play out, though I am hoping it gets me some kind of an upgrade. But the truth is, for a long time I considered myself a follower because of what I knew.

I was born into a Christian home and rarely missed a weekend of church. From before I can remember I could quote the Lord's Prayer, John 3:16, and the 23rd Psalm. When I was around five years old I threw a fit because my mom was making me wear a tie to church. She was trying to understand why I was so upset, and through my tears

I explained, "If I wear a tie they might make me preach!" By the age of thirteen I felt pressure to have the "Baptist blow-dry" hairstyle that my father was somewhat of a legend for perfecting. I would regularly wear the latest in "witness wear." When I was in junior high I even had a picture of Jesus hanging on my wall right next to the poster of Michael Jordan. In some ways that is a visual example of how I would define my relationship with Jesus at the time. I was a fan of Jesus, like I was a fan of Mike. I had memorized his records and knew his stats, but I did not know him.

If you would have confronted me on being just a fan of Jesus and not a completely committed follower I would have defended myself by trying to challenge you to "sword drill." That's where you see who can turn to a Scripture reference the fastest.* I would point to my impressive record whenever I competed in a "quote off." A "quote off" is similar to a "dance off" except you quote Bible verses. As I grew older I would have pointed to the religious traditions I followed and the moral code I observed as evidence that I was a follower of Jesus. I would have filled you in on the fact that I don't drink. I would have let you know that I've never said a cussword, at least not loud enough to be heard. In fact, my friends and I were such committed followers, we made up Christian cusswords.

If you really had pushed me I would have had to break out the Spiritual Leadership Award I won at a Christian basketball camp. I may have pulled out the ribbon I won for getting runner-up for camper of the week at church camp. I would have also explained that I got ripped off because the kid who got first place was the camp dean's son, or, as I like to call him, a cheating S.O.D. (Son of the Dean). Instead of describing a relationship where I truly knew Jesus, I would have told you what I knew about Jesus. But when there is knowledge without intimacy, you're really no more than a fan.

---

* If you didn't know that, I would so dominate you.

knowledge about him or intimacy with him?

Yada, Yada, Yada

Probably the best biblical word for intimacy is the word "know." But this knowing goes much deeper than knowledge. The Bible first uses this word to describe a relationship in Genesis 4:1:

Adam **knew** Eve his wife (KJV).

The Hebrew word for "knew" here is the word *yada'*. Here's the best way to define the word *yada'*:

To know completely and to be completely known.

But the NIV translates the word a little differently, because it puts it in context of what's happening. So your Bible probably says in Genesis 4:1:

Adam lay with his wife Eve.

You get the picture? That is our context for yada'. Now don't just giggle and brush past this. This is not just a "yada, yada, yada" moment, okay? This is a YADA' moment between a husband and a wife. It's this intimate connection on every level. To know and to be known completely. It's a beautiful picture that helps us get at what it really means to know Christ. There are other Hebrew words that could have been used to describe the sexual intimacy that is taking place. These words for sex are used later in Scripture and refer to the physical act or even procreation. But the word in Genesis 4 is *yada'*, the Hebrew word for "know." Clearly when the Bible uses this word for "know" it means much more than knowledge. It describes the most intimate of connections. One Hebrew scholar defines the word this way: "A mingling of the souls." That's more than knowledge, that's intimacy.

So now you understand that this word translated "know" is used to describe a man and a woman being intimate with one another. They *yada'* each other. With that in mind I want to talk to you about how God wants to know and be known by us. What I'm about to tell you will seem a little bit strange to some of you, a little bit weird. I get that. We can work through some of the weirdness, but I at least wanted to give you a heads-up going into it.*

If you trace the usage of yada' through the Old Testament, you'll find that over and over again, this is the same word that's used to describe God's relationship with us. Over and over, yada' is the word that's used to describe how God wants to be known by you. In fact, that's the way he already knows you. In Psalm 139 David uses this word a half dozen times to describe how God knows us:

> O Lord, you have examined my heart and know everything about me. You know when I sit down or stand up. You know my thoughts even when I'm far away. You see me when I travel and when I rest at home. You know everything I do. You know what I am going to say even before I say it, Lord (NLT).

Think about that! The same word, the same connection used to describe a man and a wife is used to describe how God knows you and how he wants to be *known* by you. This completely changed the way I defined my relationship with Jesus. I began to see what he wanted from me as a follower. Instead of identifying myself as a follower because I know *about* Jesus, I understand that I am a follower because I know Jesus.

In Luke 7, the Pharisee knew all about Jesus, but didn't know Jesus. His heart was far from him. He didn't know that the visiting rabbi sitting at his table was the promised Messiah that he had spent countless hours studying about. Luke tells us that while Jesus is eating at this Pharisee's house a woman comes on the scene. They were likely eating in a courtyard area where people could watch and even listen in on the conversation. But things start to get awkward when this woman comes uninvited up to the table where they are eating. To better comprehend the tension of this moment, understand that this wasn't just any woman. Verse 37 tells us that she was a "sinner."

---

* The warning may be unnecessary, but in middle school I was blindsided by the sex ed class. Seems like my mom and dad should have given me some kind of advance notice. Something like, "Hey son, heads-up, today your creepy math teacher will scar you for life when he explains where babies come from."

More specifically, she was a known prostitute in the village. She must have heard Jesus teaching, maybe earlier in the day, and something happened in her heart.

What was Jesus teaching on that had such an impact? Forgiveness? Perhaps as she sat and listened to Jesus her eyes welled up with tears as she realized that God loved her and wanted to forgive her. Redemption? Maybe as Jesus spoke she realized that God could put back together the broken pieces of her life. But then again, maybe it wasn't what Jesus taught. Maybe it was the way he looked at her. His eyes communicated her value and worth. She wasn't just a "sinner" to him; she was a beloved daughter. And perhaps when Jesus finished teaching she knew God loved her and he hadn't given up on her, even if everyone else had. And she must have whispered something like this to herself: *Maybe it's not too late for me. Maybe even someone like me can follow him.*

She was desperate to see Jesus again, and she overheard someone saying that he was having dinner at the home of Simon the Pharisee —a dinner she would never be invited to attend, not in a thousand years. Of course, normally she would have no interest in attending. She had felt the condemning glares of the Pharisees enough to stay as far away as possible from places like Simon's house. But she had to see Jesus. It's hard to imagine what it would take for her to walk into that courtyard. But she is so focused on Jesus that she forgets about herself. She is desperate to express the love and affection she feels for him. What she does next is reckless, it's impulsive, it's inappropriate, and it's exactly the kind of follower Jesus wants.

Picture the scene. Jesus is reclining at the table. Instead of using chairs they would lean on an elbow that was propped up by a cushion. Their feet would be away from the table. This woman approaches and stands at the filthy feet of Jesus. The table grows silent. Everybody is watching. Everybody knows who she is. *What is she doing?* She looks around at the guests. She feels from some that familiar glare of condemnation. Others keep their eyes down, embarrassed by her presence and the awkwardness of the moment. But when she looks at Jesus, he seems to know what has happened in her heart. He gives her a warm smile. He seems delighted that she has come, and he looks at her with the eyes of a loving father watching his beautiful daughter as she enters the room. She has never had a man look at her that way before. She is so undone by this that the tears come, just a few at first, and then more. She falls to the ground and begins to kiss his feet. Soon, the tears are just pouring down her face. They begin to drip onto the dirty feet of Jesus. As she looks at the muddy streaks she suddenly realizes that his feet haven't been washed. She can't ask for a towel, so she lets down her hair. In those days women always wore their hair up in public. For a woman to wear her hair down in front of a man that was not her husband was considered to be such an intimate expression that it was literally grounds for divorce. When she did this there was likely an audible gasp. She begins washing the feet of Jesus with her tears and drying them with her hair.

Then Luke says she had an alabaster jar of ointment. Most likely this refers to a flask that was often worn around the neck as a kind of perfume for women. As you might guess, because of her profession, this flask was quite important. She had used it a drop at a time many, many times, for many men. But now she empties it. She just empties the whole thing out. She will not need it anymore. She pours this flask, her life, on his feet, and she kisses them over and over. At the end of the story Jesus says to Simon:

> Look at this woman kneeling here. When I entered your home, you didn't offer me water to wash the dust from my feet, but she has washed them with her tears and wiped them with her hair. You didn't greet me with a kiss, but from the time I first came in, she has not stopped kissing my feet. You neglected the courtesy of olive oil to anoint my head, but she has anointed my feet with rare perfume.
>
> Luke 7:44–46 NLT

In the end the religious leader with all the knowledge is the fan, and the prostitute who intimately expressed her love for Jesus is shown to be the follower. Here, then, is the question you and I have to ask ourselves:

knowledge about him or intimacy with him?

Who am I most like in the story?

Have you ever had a moment with Jesus like this woman in Luke 7 had? When's the last time you've poured yourself out before him? When is the last time the tears streamed down your face as you expressed your love for him? When is the last time you demonstrated your love for him with reckless abandonment?

I am not asking if you know about him, I am asking if you know him.

not a fan story

Sarah Hartman

When I was a young girl, I started playing experimental games of "truth or dare" with a close female friend. The guilt of these experiences scarred me deeply. I struggled at just eleven years old with tremendous, unrelenting guilt. I can remember the first time I thought of suicide. Dying scared me so much that I told my mom about the truth or dare incidents. Despite my confession and my mother's reassurance, I could not forgive myself. Time passed, but my guilt and shame did not. My freshman year of high school was a major adjustment for me. My guilt and sadness gave way to total madness, and I went into a very deep depression. By the time I confided in someone who could help, I had already begun cutting myself and was hopeless and suicidal. While my mother desperately continued praying for me, I saw doctors and therapists. They prescribed all kinds of treatments and medications, but never reached my heart with the mercy of God. I was always a tear-streaked mess at school, barely surviving the day. I was behaving irrationally and having abnormal panic attacks. What I had been raised to believe about God and biblical truth was replaced with lies that I could do whatever I wanted and be fine. My sophomore year of high school, I came out as a lesbian, and kept it from my family. I was telling horrible lies and hated my mother. She never gave up on me. She fought for me, because I wasn't fighting for myself. Throughout my junior and senior years, I continued to battle depression, gained weight, believed lies, and lived in guilt over my past. All this time, I never dealt with the real issue of needing to know Jesus. I just couldn't accept, after what I had done, that he loved me. Then toward the end of my senior year, God led me to counselors and teachers who became his healing for me.

His truth reached my heart through their love and acceptance. It is through God working a miracle in my life that I am free of who I was a few years ago. My life is so different now that I can't believe that this story is about me. I recently married a wonderful Christian man, and have never looked back on who I was, except to remember how God has rescued me. My name is Sarah Hartman and I am not a fan.

one of many or your one and only?

Luke 14

In the fourteenth chapter of Luke's gospel Jesus has another D.T.R. talk, but this time it isn't one on one in the shadows of the night, or sitting around a dinner table. This time Jesus speaks to an entire crowd. By this point in Jesus' life, word had spread about this incredible teacher who made the lame walk, the blind see, and who turned funeral processions into family reunions. People were coming from all over and filling the hillsides. I imagine the scenes really did have the atmosphere of a stadium full of raving fans.

For a while Jesus seemed okay with the large crowds. He was fine with people coming out to be inspired by his teaching. He didn't seem to mind the fact that they were coming to see some miracles. No doubt many of them showed up carrying popcorn with extra butter, ready for the entertainment to begin. Jesus welcomed people who were curious and wanting to find out more about this unconventional rabbi. But the time comes when he wants to talk about the relationship. He draws a line in the sand and wants to know where these people stand. Ultimately what concerned Jesus the most wasn't the size of the crowd, it was the level of commitment.

Have they just come for a miracle and healing show? Do they just want to hear a motivational speaker? We're about to find out because this crowd is going to be separated into two groups: fans and followers.

Large crowds were traveling with Jesus, and turning to them he said:

"If anyone comes to me and does not hate his father and mother, his wife and children, his brothers and sisters—yes, even his own life—he cannot be my disciple" (Luke 14:25–26).

That doesn't seem very seeker sensitive at all. You would think it would read:

A large crowd was following Jesus. He turned around and said to them, "What a great crowd! I want everyone to go invite one friend and come back tonight for a carnival. We'll have live music. All the loaves and fish you can eat. We'll even have a 'water to wine' booth. I may even get in the dunk booth. And whoever invites the most friends gets one free miracle. Let's pack this hillside out!"

Instead he tells the people that if they want to follow him, they must hate their family, even their own lives.

What the what?

Where did that come from? I'm sure that about this time, some of the fans began to pack up and head home. It was fun while it lasted, but this isn't what they signed up for.

Some teachers have tried to soften these words of Jesus by saying they were only meant for a select few who would specifically be chosen to represent him. In other words, Jesus was only speaking to the seminary students and full-time ministers. Everyone can take a deep breath. That was a close call but he wasn't talking to you. But it says "large crowds." And when Jesus speaks to the "large crowds" he doesn't address a specific segment. In fact, the word for *crowd* here simply means, "a large group of unidentified people." He wasn't singling out a specific group. Did you notice the word he used in verse 26? Jesus says, "If *anyone* ..." That's a fairly inclusive word. Jesus isn't laying out the entrance requirements for the twelve disciples. He is not talking to a seminary class. He's not addressing a group of pastors and missionaries. He's not just talking to kids who grew up in the church and professed their faith when they were ten. He's not just speaking to Bible Bowl team. Jesus didn't have one message that he preached at the National Youth Workers convention and another message he preached to the seekers on the hillside. What Jesus says is true for anyone who wants to follow him.

So the big question is, *Does following Jesus really mean that you have to hate your nanna?**

Obviously, hating your family would contradict the other teachings of Jesus. So why the strong language? Maybe Jesus uses such dramatic language here because in this culture if you were to become a follower of Jesus without your family's blessing, you would have been thought of as hating your family. A decision to follow Jesus would have been interpreted as turning your back on your family and walking away from them. Some of you understand.

A college student caught me after a church service and told me with big tears in her eyes that she had given her life to Jesus. After I expressed my excitement for her decision, she told me that she wanted to be baptized. I assumed she was planning on being baptized at some point in the future. I told her I would look forward to celebrating that moment with her. She spoke again, but this time there was a greater sense of urgency in her voice. She said, "No, you don't understand. I want to be baptized right now."

A few minutes later we were backstage getting ready to step into the water and she seemed a little bit nervous. In an effort to help her feel more confident I asked her, "Do you have any family or friends out there to cheer you on?" She said no and then she added, "My parents are not going to be happy about this." She looked down and took a deep breath. She walked out in front of me and stepped into the water. Fans don't do that. Fans are not willing to follow Jesus if it means disappointing their family. When their relationship with Jesus starts to hurt their relationships with others, that's asking too much.

Jesus is honest with the crowd about what it may cost to follow him. He lets them know that following him may mean offending your parents or grandparents. It may mean being cut out of the will or even cut off from the family. I've talked to people who put off following Jesus

---
* Aka: Grandma/Granny/Grammy/Meemaw/Mammo/Mimi/Mamaw, etc.

because they don't want to hurt their parents' feelings. I have had more than one person tell me that when their grandma dies they plan on becoming a Christian. They decide to wait for now because they don't want to upset her.

And maybe as you sit in the crowd it seems that Jesus is talking directly to you. You know that your dad won't approve. He'll roll his eyes and mumble something about you getting carried away. Your brother or sister won't know what to make of your decision to follow and they may distance themselves from you. Your boyfriend or girlfriend may very well break up with you. You can hear your friends laughing behind your back about you finding religion. And Jesus is saying, "Yep, that may be part of it. And if you're not willing to choose me over your family, then you are not ready to follow, and maybe it's time for you to go on home."

The word *hate* is defined as "to dislike something intensely" or to have "feelings of intense hostility." Clearly Jesus doesn't want us to "hate" our family in that sense. It would violate everything else the Bible teaches on the subject. Jesus himself said one of the two greatest commandments was, "Love your neighbor as yourself." Our families are the closest neighbors we have. It's helpful to read how the New Living Translation version of the Bible puts it:

> If you want to be my disciple, you must hate everyone else by comparison—your father and mother, wife and children, brothers and sisters ... (Luke 14:26 NLT).

The NLT says "hate" but then adds "everyone else by comparison." The *Contemporary English Version* says "love me more." The most accurate understanding of what Jesus is requiring of his followers is a combination of these two translations. Jesus is most likely conveying the idea of "love me more," but "hate" is also accurate, because it captures the degree to which we love Jesus more.

Imagine that the different loves of your life are competing in a race to see who wins first place. Picture in your mind who would be at the starting line of this race. You mom, maybe your dad, you best friends, your boyfriend or girlfriend; even a sibling has made the cut.

Jesus is there too. In fact, you've given him the inside lane, so he has some advantage. The idea isn't that Jesus comes in first place in this race. What Jesus is describing here is more accurately understood by picturing a race for first place in your life and he is the only one on the track. Jesus isn't just saying, "I want to be first place in your life." He is saying, "I don't even want there to be a second place." When we compare our relationship with him to anyone else there should be no competition. Fans will try and make Jesus one of many. Some fans may even make Jesus the first of many. But when Jesus defines the relationship he makes it clear; he wants to be your one and only.

Diagnosing Fandom —
QUESTION 3: Is Jesus One of Many or Is He Your One and Only?

So picture yourself in the future sitting down and having the D.T.R. talk with someone special. You've been dating for a while and you are ready to define the relationship and determine the level of commitment. You start off the talk and try to make it clear where you stand. You are all-in. You make it clear that you want nothing more than to spend the rest of your life with this person. The tears well up in your eyes as you say those three words: *I love you.* Now imagine that your significant other returns the words of affection and says *I love you too and I want to spend the rest of my life with you.* You breathe a sigh of relief. But then you hear this caveat: *I just have one condition. I still want to see other people.*

That is essentially what a fan says to Jesus. A fan says, *I love you. I am committed to you. But let's not be exclusive.* Or guys, imagine that after you have the D.T.R. talk you carry your girlfriend's picture in your wallet. As soon as it's opened, her picture is the first thing you see. When she opens your wallet and sees her picture she thinks it's sweet, but imagine that behind her picture are pictures of the last three or four girls you have dated. That's going to be a problem. It's not enough for her to be first; she will insist on being "the only." Jesus makes it clear that he will not share your affection. Following him requires your whole heart.

I want to ask you some questions to help reveal if Jesus is one of many, or your one and only. These are not rhetorical questions. Take time to answer them. Grab a pen and write your answers in the space below each question. How you answer these questions can help show you what is competing with Jesus for your affection.

1. What do you sacrifice your money for? The Bible says, "Where your treasure is, there your heart will be also." What you spend your time and money on often reveals the true desire of your heart and shows who or what you are truly following. The reason Jesus talked more about money than any other subject is because it can easily become his chief competition. We end up following money and the things money can buy instead of Jesus.

Many of us sacrifice our time and money for stuff because we think that's how we find satisfaction. For many, satisfaction comes with a price tag. If you just had enough money you could order it off the internet or buy it off the shelf. But Jesus wants to be our satisfaction. He described himself as living water that quenches our thirst forever. Money becomes a substitute for God because it promises to do for us what he wants to do for us.

In Matthew 6:24 Jesus said, "No one can serve two masters. Either he will hate the one and love the other, or he will be devoted to the one and despise the other. You cannot serve both God and Money." You can't follow money and Jesus. Those paths go in different directions and you have to choose one.

As a pastor I've done some financial counseling over the years, and I have noticed a common way that fans will talk about their finances. A fan will ask "What's the most I can spend on my house?" But when it comes to giving they'll ask, "Does God want me to give to him out of net income or my gross income?" In other words, "What's the most I can spend on my house, and the least I can give to God?" How you spend your money tells a story about what matters the most to you.

I know some students will think that this question is one they will answer when they get a little older and make some real money. But now is the time to make it clear what your priority will be. The Bible teaches that what we do with a little is a clear indication of what we will do if we ever have a lot. Your bank account may very well offer the best evidence as to whether you are a fan or a follower.

2. When you're hurt, where do you go for comfort? When you experience the pain of this life, where do you turn? Maybe it's to a parent or a best friend. Maybe it's to the refrigerator. Isn't that why they call it comfort food?* Do you bury yourself in school work, music, sports, or video games? All these things have the potential to compete with Jesus for our devotion and affection. There is certainly nothing wrong with finding comfort from family and friends; that's part of God's design. There is nothing wrong with being passionate about sports or music. But the question is, "Do these people or things take the place of Jesus?"

I have found that when someone goes through a difficult time or a painful circumstance, who or what they are truly following is often revealed. When our first response to suffering is to turn to anyone or anything other than Jesus it may reveal that our affection is divided and we are following someone or something other than Jesus.

Imagine that a mother visits the school where her kindergarten son attends. The mother has felt a little bit threatened because her son loves his new teacher and talks about her constantly. During recess the mother stands next to the teacher and discusses her child's progress. Her little boy is swinging from the monkey bars and falls hard. He gets up crying and runs towards his mom and teacher. Now the little boy loves his teacher, but when he approaches them, to whom will he look for comfort? He wouldn't have to stop and think; he

---

* I find a frozen pizza followed by Oreo ice cream to be extremely comforting. Like a mother's warm embrace.

would run into his mom's arms. Do you see what happened? The pain he experienced created an honest moment where his true affection was revealed.

So when is the last time you experienced some of the pain and suffering of this life? You didn't make the team, a friend stabbed you in the back, a relationship ended, you found out that you have some health problems, you parents told you that they were getting a divorce. When you experienced the pain, where did you turn? The answer to that question reveals your heart's true devotion.

3. What disappoints or frustrates you the most? When we feel overwhelmed with disappointment it often reveals something that has become too important. It may be something as insignificant as failing a test or losing a ball game. When we find that those things have the power to determine who we are and what kind of day we have, it very well may be evidence that something is more important than it should be. Of course some level of disappointment and frustration can be natural. But if you find that you are excessively disappointed or over-frustrated, it's an indication of what might be competing for affection that is to be Christ's alone.

Imagine a child who is excited that his father is going to take him fishing. As the day goes on the fish just aren't biting. The more time passes, the more frustrated and disappointed the father becomes. On the drive home he is silent, but clearly upset. Isn't that an indication that the most important part of the day for the father wasn't spending time with his child, but catching fish?

Do you see how excessive disappointment and constant frustration can reveal a heart's true passion? You may need some help answering this question objectively. Ask a close friend or family member what seems to disappoint or frustrate you. If you hear answers like when your favorite team loses, or when you have a bad hair day, or when you find out your favorite TV show got deleted, it may reveal that something is out of order.

4. What gets you really excited? Recently I was watching a college football game on TV when my twelve-year-old daughter came in and said, "I've never seen you so excited." She has seen me baptize new believers. She saw my reaction to the birth of her baby brother. She has seen me take her out for many daddy/daughter dates. But she has never seen me more excited than watching a college football game. *Ouch.*

Like the things that disappoint us, the things that excite us can also point to something or someone that is in competition with Jesus. The things that make the list when you answer the question of what gets you excited can easily be things that are fine and good, but they have the potential to become a substitute for God in your heart.

Following Jesus means following him alone. Fans don't want to put Jesus on the throne of their hearts. Instead they keep a couch on their hearts and, at the most, give Jesus a cushion. He's asked to share the space. But Jesus makes it clear to this crowd he's not interested in sharing your heart.

So in Luke 14 Jesus defines the relationship by making it clear that if we follow him, we follow him and him alone. He won't share you —not with money, not with a hobby, not even with your family. Maybe you read a passage like this and it seems that God is being a little possessive and jealous. But understand this—when Jesus explains that he will not share your affection or devotion, he isn't just saying how he wants to be loved by you; he is making it clear how he loves you.

Imagine it this way. (This is strictly pretend.) Let's imagine that this week you walk into a restaurant and you see me sitting at a table having a candlelit dinner with a woman who is not my wife. You come up and confront me, saying, "Who is this woman and what are you doing?"

I respond, "Don't worry about it. I am on a date with this beautiful lady tonight, but my wife knows that she always comes first." You walk away angry and disgusted. You decide that someone needs to tell my wife and so you call her and break the news.

When I come home from my date, what do you think her response will be? Imagine my wife meets me at the door and says, "Hi, honey, did you have a nice time on your date?" Then she comes over and gives me a big kiss and says, "I don't mind you seeing other people as long as I am most important to you."

That would never happen! As soon as I walked in the door from the date I would fear for my life. If my wife heard about me eating at McDonald's with a man who kind of looked like a woman, I would be in trouble.* Why? Because she loves me. Her refusal to share my affection doesn't indict her as insecure and possessive; instead it proves her to be devoted and loving.

And Jesus makes it clear: if you follow him, he is to be your one and only. You're so committed to him that by comparison, you hate everyone else.

I can't help but wonder how the disciples responded to teaching like this in Luke 14. Perhaps they would get pretty upset with Jesus for teaching such things. Talk about a momentum killer. A sermon where a main point is "Hate your mom" has a way of turning people off. That's not what we call a crowd pleaser. The disciples must have cringed when Jesus began one of these sermons, knowing that they would lose influence with the people.

On the other hand, maybe the disciples didn't mind so much. They had given up everything to follow Jesus, and I'm sure they had come

---

* This is not part of the imagining. I did eat out once with a guy who kind of looked like a girl and my wife questioned me. His name was Blair, which certainly didn't help the situation.

to realize that this is the only way it could work. Trying to follow Jesus part-time or halfhearted is impossible. The relationship he wants with you requires your whole heart. And fans should know that his terms are not negotiable. So before you say, "I want to be a follower," be sure you understand what it's going to cost you.

Jesus continues to teach the crowd in Luke 14. And he seems to give an explanation of why he is teaching in such a direct and straightforward way:

> Suppose one of you wants to build a tower. Will he not first sit down and estimate the cost to see if he has enough money to complete it? For if he lays the foundation and is not able to finish it, everyone who sees it will ridicule him, saying, "This fellow began to build and was not able to finish" (Luke 14:28–30).

Jesus makes no apologies for his strong words. He wants people to be clear about what they are signing on for.

John Oros was a church leader in Romania during the communist era. When he spoke at the Associated Mennonite Biblical Seminary, he talked about what that was like:

> During communism, many of us preached ... and people came at the end of a service, and they said, "I have decided to become a Christian." We told them, "It is good that you want to become a Christian, but we would like to tell you that there is a price to be paid. Why don't you reconsider what you want to do, because many things can happen to you. You can lose, and you can lose big."

John said that a high percentage of them chose to take part in a three-month class to better understand the decision they were making. John says:

> At the end of this period, many participants declared their desire to be baptized. Typically, I would respond, "It's really nice that you want to become a Christian, but when you give your testimony, there will be informers here who will jot down your name. Tomorrow the problems will start. Count the cost. Christianity is not easy. It's not cheap. You can be demoted. You can lose your job. You can lose your friends. You

can lose your neighbors. You can lose your kids. You can lose even your own life."

He wanted the people to get to a place where following Jesus was so important to them, if they lost everything it would still be worth it.

That's a lot different than the invitation to which many of us responded. At the end of the sermon the preacher said something like, "I want everybody to bow their heads and close their eyes. If you want to become a Christian then just raise your hand ... I see that hand ... I see that hand ..." But Jesus makes it clear that you need to count the cost.

Let me ask you the question this way: If following Jesus cost you everything, would it still be worth it?

not a fan story

Josh Doolin

I grew up in the church, and went to a Christian school. From the start, I was expected to look a certain way and do certain things. My parents loved the Lord and wanted to be sure I did too. Ever since I can remember I had been taught that Jesus is the only way to heaven, he loves me and died for me, and I must follow him. However, how to follow him never really got explained much beyond what not to do. The way I saw following was to wear "Jesus accessories" and keep my shirt tucked in, and always have good manners and make wise choices. Up until high school, I believed that God had set the bar, and if I was going to get into heaven I better not fall short.

In middle school there were so many temptations around me. I remember feeling so much guilt after seeing a TV show that I wasn't supposed to watch, or looking at a girl in a bikini on the internet. I was constantly afraid God would erase me from the "list." I tried so hard to hold onto the Christian lifestyle by following rules, but found myself incomplete. I saw God using other people in incredible ways, but never saw him doing anything in my life. I was sure I wasn't following "hard enough," so I would try harder not to mess up. But trying wasn't working.

I began to please people since I didn't believe I could please God. Wherever I could feel accepted is where I went. I got good grades to be accepted by teachers, I helped out at home to be accepted by my parents, but most of all I wanted to be accepted by my friends. I was shy, but I had a deep longing to be part of the in-crowd. I hoped that my acceptance from these people would make me feel better, but it didn't. I was terrible at fitting in. I was extremely awkward and couldn't last two minutes (even two seconds) talking to a girl. I just wanted someone with open arms to reach out and take all the stress away. Someone who would love me for me, as awkward and insecure as I was.

The year I started high school, the Lord answered my prayer and led me to a close friend who accepted me. He had a true relationship with Jesus. We were both calling ourselves Christians, but he wasn't overly exhausted like I was. He was secure and sure of who he was in Christ. He showed me that you don't have to have it all together to come to Jesus. I slowly learned that Jesus loves me where I am, and no amount of rule keeping is going to make him accept me any more than he already does. Now, during my senior year, God is showing me that he wants me to become a pastor. I am going on my third mission trip, and loving others the way he has loved me. By dying to myself — my old, shy, desperate, lonely, and people-pleasing self — and allowing him to be Lord of my life, God has truly made me complete.

My name is Josh Doolin, and I am not a fan.

following jesus
or following the rules?

Matthew 23

In 2004, Matt Emmons was one shot away from claiming victory in the Olympics. He was competing in the 50-meter three-position rifle event. He didn't even need a bull's-eye to win. His final shot merely needed to be on target. Normally, the shot he made would have received a score of 8.1, more than enough for a gold medal. But in what was described as "an extremely rare mistake in elite competition," Emmons fired at the wrong target. Standing in lane two, he fired at the target in lane three. His score for a good shot at the wrong target: 0. Instead of a medal, Emmons ended up in eighth place.

That's a picture of what happens to a lot of fans. If you asked them, "Are you a fan or a follower?" they would confidently respond "follower." It's not a question of their effort or desire. They are following hard. Here is the problem; it's not Jesus they are following. Without realizing it, they are aiming at the wrong target. Instead of following Jesus, fans often follow religious rules and rituals. They have confused the targets.

In Matthew 23, Jesus tries to get the attention of a group of fans known as the religious leaders. If you were trying to determine who were the fans and who were the followers in Jesus' day, it would be likely that these religious leaders would quickly be identified as the followers. They had a mastery of the Scriptures and were considered expert theologians. They were especially known for their strict observance of the law. They would have received high scores for their religious rule keeping, but that's not the target Jesus was most concerned about. Following the rules kept them focused on the outside, but who they were on the inside is what Jesus paid attention to. And the problem with these religious leaders is that, like many fans, who they were on the outside didn't match up with what was on the inside. In this chapter Jesus preaches one of his last sermons here on earth and it's directed right at these religious leaders. He doesn't hold anything back. If you grew up thinking of Jesus as a Mr. Rogers of Nazareth who was always smiling, winking at people, and wearing a sweater vest, the tone Jesus takes with these religious leaders may surprise you. The name of the sermon we're going to study is not "Won't You Be My Neighbor?" This sermon is traditionally called "The Seven Woes."

The word "woe" is an onomatopoeia—a word where the definition comes from its sound.* The word "woe" is both an expression of grief and a curse. Seven times in his sermon Jesus says, "Woe to you ..." Each "woe" is followed by a scathing rebuke. This isn't a warning by Jesus. He isn't cautioning the religious leaders. He isn't offering them counsel or advice. Jesus is strongly opposing these religious leaders because he doesn't want people to confuse following the rules with following him. His indictments against these religious leaders should serve as a warning to those fans who consider themselves followers because of their religious rule keeping and Christian credentials.

The Fan Club

These spiritual leaders Jesus is addressing in Matthew 23 made up a religious ruling body of seventy-two men called the Sanhedrin. Within the Sanhedrin there were two different groups, called the Sadducees and the Pharisees. These two groups did not get along. When interpreting Scripture the Sadducees were very liberal, and the Pharisees were quite conservative. The Sadducees served the roles of Chief Priests and Elders. If you were a Sadducee, it meant you were

---

* Other onomatopoeias that would be difficult to work into the title of a sermon: *buzz*, *beep*, *click*, *clack*, *fizz*, *whoosh*, *slurp*, *swish*, and *plop*.

born into that position. There were, of course, other requirements, but it had to be part of your heritage. But to be a part of the Pharisees, your qualifications weren't based on the family you were born into; it was your hard work. Becoming a Pharisee required an incredible amount of textual study and theological training. And what I've noticed is that many fans fit into one of these two camps.

Some fans are like the Sadducees. Their faith was something they were born into. It was never really something they chose. Maybe when you were born your parents handed you a mask, and you grew up acting like Christians act, talking how Christians talked, listening to the music Christians listened to; but you never fell in love with Jesus. Your faith has always been more about honoring your heritage than surrendering your heart.

On the other hand, some fans are like the Pharisees. They would measure their faith by their hard work at learning and following the law. Their intellectual knowledge and behavioral compliance was the target they were aiming at. But even though they were saying the right things and doing the right things, it wasn't a reflection of who they really were. You may say the right things and do the right things, but that's not enough for Jesus. He wants all of you.

Your faith has always been more about honoring your heritage than surrendering your heart.

I was waiting in the aisle of the grocery store when the cover of *People* magazine caught my eye. It was a picture of the famous tennis player, Andre Agassi. For years he was one of the top players in the world. He turned pro when he was sixteen and won eight Grand Slams over the span of his twenty-year career. The headline said "My Secret Life." I picked it up and began to read. The article was about his autobiography *Open*. It turns out he doesn't really like tennis. He never did. In fact, he hated it during his growing up years and through most of his career. He writes: "My dad decided before I was born that I would be the number one player in the world." In the article he describes a practice session at age seven: "My arm feels like it's about to fall off. I ask, 'How much longer, Pops?' No answer. I get an idea. Accidentally, on purpose I hit a ball high over the fence.

I catch it on the rim of the racket so it sounds like a misfire. My father sees the ball leave the court and curses. He stomps out of the yard. I now have four and a half minutes to catch my breath." Maybe the most telling sentence in that article was this one. Agassi says, "I never chose this life." On the outside you would never guess his heart wasn't in it. He's put in countless hours of practice. He's battled for championships. He was really good at what he did. But he was wearing a mask. Because he never chose it, it was never his. As a result there was no love.[1]

And this describes many fans that I know. You look really good. You have this part down. You know what to say, and what not to say. You can pray the prayers and you can sing the songs. But you never chose it. It was just handed down to you. Or you're going through the motions, putting on an impressive performance, but it isn't real. Your heart is not in it.

Diagnosing Fandom — QUESTION 4: **Are You More Focused on the Outside Than the Inside?**

The main problem Jesus had with these religious leaders is they were hypocrites. I'm not guessing at that, that's what he calls them. To their faces. Eight times. The word *hypocrite* comes from Greek ancient classical theater. Greek actors were called *hypocrites*. Often, a single actor would play several different characters, and for each character, the actor would use a different mask. So when they would switch characters, they would switch masks. Kind of like Tyler Perry or Adam Sandler attempting to play different characters in the same film. So in Greek theater one person might play all the different parts. Each character uses a different mask but you never really see the actor's face. The actor is always behind one of these masks. Because fans tend to get caught up on what people see on the outside, they almost always find themselves wearing a mask. What people see doesn't reflect who they really are. Jesus says in verse 5:

> Everything they do is for show (NLT).

As a recovering hypocrite, I can tell you that some fans can be almost impossible to identify because they deliver Oscar-worthy performances as they play the role of a follower. When Jesus begins his sermon in Matthew 23 he is speaking to the people about the religious leaders while they listen in:

> Then Jesus said to the crowds and to his disciples: "The teachers of the law and the Pharisees sit in Moses' seat. So you must obey them and do everything they tell you" (vv. 1 – 3a).

I wonder if Jesus paused here for a moment. The Pharisees think, "Okay, this is more like it. He's finally coming over to our side. He's pointing to us as the authorities." But Jesus continues:

> But do not do what they do, for they do not practice what they preach (v. 3b).

The problem that Jesus had with these teachers is that what they were teaching wasn't a reflection of who they really were.

These religious types were the fans that Jesus seems to have the most trouble with. Fans who will walk into a restaurant and bow their heads to pray before a meal just in case someone is watching. Fans who won't go to certain movies at the theater, but will watch the same movie online when no one else is around. Fans who may feed the hungry and help the needy, and then they make sure they work it into every conversation for the next two weeks. Fans who go to that party Saturday night and then show up to church Sunday morning a little hungover. Fans who open up the Bible app on their phone and read along during the message and then later that evening use the same phone to watch porn. Fans who spend several hours staring in the mirror getting ready for the day to make sure they look perfect on the outside, but who can't find the time to spend ten minutes examining what's on the inside. Fans who like seeing other people fail because in their minds it makes them look better. Fans whose primary concern is what other people think. Fans who are reading this and assuming I'm describing someone else. Fans who have worn the mask for so long they have fooled even themselves.

Jesus has harsh words for these fans who were trying to impress others through their religious credentials. It's interesting to note that as severe as Jesus was with these religious leaders he is just as tender and encouraging to those who have genuinely given him their hearts, even if they don't have it all together on the outside. Please don't miss this: Jesus doesn't expect followers to be perfect, but he does call them to be authentic.

Every week I get a chance to sit down with the people who are new to our church. On any given week there are anywhere from two to twenty people sitting around a table. They have a chance to tell their story, and I have an opportunity to listen and pray for them. Typically we have two separate kinds of people in that room. There are some who have been around the church and God for a while. They know the rules. They know what to say and how to say it. They know what words to include and what parts of their stories to leave out. They've learned to wear a mask.

Then there are those who are new to Christ and the church. They haven't learned the rules. And when they tell their story they will include a family that fell apart. It's not uncommon for their stories to begin "I've been sober for ..." and sometimes it's been years. Sometimes it's been days. They don't know any better. I've heard ex-cons talk about their crime. I've heard men of every age talk about pornography and women tell about credit card debt. Parents will talk about how much they are struggling with their kids. Kids will talk about how they've been lying to their parents and going behind their backs. They'll tell about eating disorders, gambling problems, suicide attempts, and drug addictions. They just don't know any better. And I hope nobody tells them that they're supposed to act like they've got it all together. You don't often get to see people without a mask. And it's such a beautiful thing.

That's what Christ wants in a follower — someone who isn't pretending on the outside to have it all together. That's one of the ways the word hypocrisy is defined, as "the act of pretending." When you were younger, of course, pretending was a good thing. With four young kids, we do a lot of pretending at our house. We keep an impressive and prolific costume stash in the basement. My oldest three children are girls, so we have all kinds of princess dresses, cheerleader outfits, and fairy costumes. When my son came along, he didn't have a lot to choose from. I have two sisters, but I'm the only boy in my family and I didn't want my son to suffer the way I did. To this day I have these memories* of my sisters putting me in dresses. Well, that's not going to happen to my son. Not on my watch. So last year after Halloween, when the costumes were on clearance, I decided to right this wrong. I bought a Spider-Man and Superman costume.† But I didn't stop there; I bought the Transformer Optimus Prime and the Incredible Hulk. And then I thought, *As long as I'm here I might as well get some for my son, too.* When I finally left the store I had nine different costumes. And he loves to play pretend. Pretending is something we may never grow out of. But somewhere along the way it stops being a childhood game of make-believe and we start to take our pretending a little more seriously . . . or should I say religiously. As children we may *play* pretend—but the problem Jesus had with these religious leaders is that they were *professional* pretenders.

In verses 27–28 Jesus goes on to say:

> You are like whitewashed tombs, which look beautiful on the outside but on the inside are full of dead men's bones and everything unclean. In the same way, on the outside you appear to people as righteous but on the inside you are full of hypocrisy . . .

That would often describe the faith of a fan. On the inside their faith has grown cold and is dying, but they are determined to keep up appearances. A few years ago when there was a commercial for a pharmaceutical company that was trying to sell this prescription drug for hepatitis C. My understanding is that if you have hepatitis C, you don't see it manifested outside of the body, at least not for some time; instead it just eats your insides. And in the commercial they showed this person's face and the face becomes more and more disfigured

---

* Meaning violent flashbacks.

† In retrospect, I will say that running around the house in red tights and blue Speedos may be more damaging than the princess dress.

and marred. Then there is this caption that comes up at the end of the commercial: "If Hep C attacked your face instead of your liver, you'd do something about it." If you could see what's on the inside instead of what you're just showing everybody else on the outside, I wonder if you'd do something about it. This is what Jesus is trying to do. He's trying to get people to see what's on the inside.

Choosing Rules over a Relationship

Jesus gives a number of indicators that the outside has become more important than the inside. The first one comes in verse 13 where we read:

> Woe to you, teachers of the law and Pharisees, you hypocrites! You shut the kingdom of heaven in men's faces. You yourselves do not enter, nor will you let those enter who are trying to.

They made it hard for people to come to God. They taught that God's favor and salvation was something that had to be earned, not just by keeping God's law, but also by keeping a bunch of other laws they added to it. For example, God commanded his people to "Remember the Sabbath day by keeping it holy." That was a law established by God so his people would have a day of rest and spiritual renewal as they honored God and recognized his authority. But the religious leaders added all kinds of laws to God's law and instead of that day being restful for God's people, it became exhausting. They taught that on the Sabbath you could throw an object in the air with one hand as long as you catch it with the other. This is actually where juggling originated.* You couldn't take a bath on the Sabbath. If someone spilled something on the Sabbath, you couldn't clean it up. You were not permitted to move a chair from one place to another ... and the list went on and on.

---

* That's not true. Juggling first made an appearance in ancient Egypt somewhere between 1994 and 1781 BC. Jugglers would be used at funerals and the balls were used to represent birth, life, death, and the afterlife. I think we would all agree that juggling should be reintroduced at funerals right away.

Jesus speaks so strongly to these rule-loving religious leaders because he knows that when following him becomes about following the rules, people end up walking away from both.

I grew up going to a Christian school. It was a great school, but there were a lot of rules. You couldn't have your hair over your ears if you were a boy. Girls' skirts couldn't be more than a couple of inches above their knees. Boys had to wear collared shirts. Girls had certain rules about makeup and jewelry. Now don't misunderstand what I'm saying; I don't think any of these rules were wrong or inappropriate. I think it's fine and good for a school or parents to establish such rules or guidelines. But here's what happened—a lot of my friends didn't associate all of those rules and regulations with school. Instead they connected the rules and regulations with being a Christian. For years they identified themselves as Christians and pointed to things like their short hair and collared shirts as evidence. When they got older they didn't like the rules, and because they associated following a bunch of rules with following Jesus, they walked away from both.

> Because they associated following a bunch of rules with following Jesus, they walked away from both.

When we learn to truly follow Jesus, we find that obedience to God comes from the inside out. Submission to what God wants for our lives flows naturally out of that relationship. It's not to say that what we do or don't do doesn't matter, but what we do or don't do must come from who we are as followers of Jesus.

When I first began to drive, I studied in order to pass the test. I knew what I was getting into. I committed to the rules of the road when I got my driver's license. Rules like:

Don't speed through a yellow light.

Always use your turn signal.

Stop completely at a stop sign.

Don't pass on a solid yellow line (no matter how slow the 1988 Buick LeSabre in front of you is going).

After I got my license, I realized my parents had a whole other set of unspoken, unpublished rules that weren't on the driver's test, but clearly I was expected to keep:

> I am not to drive past my grandma's house without stopping and saying hello.
>
> I am to always turn the radio back to their easy-listening station.
>
> Sushi trash is never allowed to be put under the seat for any amount of time. (I learned to keep this one the hard way. No lie—the car smelled like rotten fish for months.)

When I turned sixteen and got my license, I loved driving. But if I saw driving as only a bunch of rules I had to keep, and not as a privilege, I would have been miserable. It's a question of what target I'm aiming at. Is my focus on the rules and restrictions or the privilege and pleasure of driving?

Is the focus of your faith on keeping a list of rules or on the privilege and pleasure of following Jesus?

Choosing Laws over Love

These religious leaders not only put rules over their relationship with Jesus, but they also were so caught up in keeping the letter of the law they didn't show love to God's people:

> Woe to you, blind guides! You say, "If anyone swears by the temple, it means nothing; but if anyone swears by the gold of the temple, he is bound by his oath." You blind fools! Which is greater: the gold, or the temple that makes the gold sacred? (vv. 16–17).

He goes on to give some other examples of how they used and abused the law. Specifically there were certain oaths that were legally binding and others that were not. So these religious fans would swear by the temple, but by the letter of the law that was invalid, so they would refuse to honor their vow. Now if they swore by the gold in the temple, then the vow had to be kept. In the Sermon on the Mount, Jesus simply taught, "Let your yes be yes and your no be no." The point of the law was for people to deal truthfully with one another, treating others with honor and respect. These religious leaders may have been keeping the letter of the law, but they were missing the spirit of it. They were technically obeying the commands of Scripture but they were missing the point of those commands. Like fans today, they would give their time and attention to following all the religious rituals, but would neglect to show God's love to the people around them, which was the point of the rules in the first place. Instead they use God's law to beat up people who are already hurting. When laws become more important than love, and rules take precedent over relationships, it's a good sign that we have become fans who are aiming at the wrong target.

My friend Steve May tells about a man named John who, dressed in blue jeans, walked into a bank to finalize a business transaction. The teller told him that the officer he needed to see wasn't in, and he would have to come back the next day. John said that would be fine and asked the teller to validate his parking ticket. The teller then informed him that, according to bank policy, she couldn't validate his parking ticket because he had not technically completed a financial transaction. John asked for an exception, since he had come to the bank intending to do business but wasn't able to because the appropriate officer wasn't in. The teller didn't budge. She said, "I'm sorry; that's our policy. Rules are rules." So John decided to make a business transaction. He decided to close his account. John's last name was Akers. He was the chairman of IBM, and the account he closed had a balance of one-and-a-half million dollars. This qualified as a financial transaction, and the teller was able to validate the parking ticket.

That is an example of how legalism works and what happens when our churches are filled with fans that make rules more important than relationships. According to the letter of the law, the bank teller was right: since no money changed hands, she didn't have to validate his parking ticket. But there's something more important than the letter of the law: the person. A number of times, the Pharisees were critical about Jesus healing a person on the Sabbath. Why? Because they were more concerned that the Sabbath be observed than they were about a person being healed. The Christian community must constantly fight the tendency to make rules and policies more important than people, because when that happens we are no longer following Jesus.

Guilt over Grace

When following the rules becomes the principal focus of a group of Christians, then you can count on guilt being the primary motivator. Jesus speaks of guilt as a weight that these religious leaders forced people to carry by making a relationship with God all about the rules. Jesus says to the Pharisees in verse 4:

> They tie up heavy loads and put them on men's shoulders.

Fans who follow the rules instead of following Jesus find that they are weighed down with guilt. Every time they come to church they find that the preacher has another weight to add to the bar. The keyword for fear and guilt is "do." We try and do enough to make up for our mistakes and earn God's favor. Instead of following Christ we are determined to make our own way. The keyword for grace is "done." Our punishment was taken by Christ. He has made a way where there was no way so we live with a freedom and an appreciation for what has been done. Fans are all about the "do," but followers celebrate the "done."

During my senior year at the Christian high school I attended, Mr. Hollingsworth was my chemistry teacher. He did something a little unusual for our last final of the year. He had been reading an article by a pastor named Charles Stanley on the grace of God and wanted to show us what grace looked like. He handed out a test to all of us that we knew would be difficult. We had been preparing for this test for several months. Before we began to take the test, he told us, "I want you to read through the entire test before you begin to take it." As we read through the test most of us realized we were in trouble. We should have studied more. But then I got to the end of the multiple-page test and read these words at the bottom: "You can try and get an A by taking this test or you can just put your name on it and automatically receive an A." This was not a difficult choice. I immediately signed my name, walked up to the desk, and headed out, thanking Charles Stanley for saving my chemistry grade. But there was a girl in our class who was the daughter of the biology teacher. She was quite intelligent and had studied hard. Apparently she got quite upset because she had spent so much time studying, and it wasn't fair that everyone else was getting an A for nothing. She stayed and took the test on principle. If she was going to get an A, she was going to earn it. And a fan says, "I'm not taking any handouts —I can do this on my own." They spend their lives carrying around the heavy burden of religion and making sure others carry that weight as well.

Fans of Jesus sooner or later find themselves exhausted. Fans grow tired of trying to maintain an outer appearance that doesn't match an inner passion. They find themselves weary of trying to keep all the rules in hopes of somehow earning God's favor. And I want you to know, before we go any further, that Jesus came to free you from religion. To those who have been hauling around a long list of rules, to those who are pretending to be more than they really are, to those who are weighed down with the fear and guilt of religion, to all the fans who are worn out on religion, Jesus invites you to follow him:

> Are you tired? Worn out? Burned out on religion? Come to me. Get away with me and you'll recover your life. I'll show you how to take a real rest. Walk with me and work with me—watch how I do it. Learn the unforced rhythms of grace. I won't lay anything heavy or ill-fitting on you. Keep company with me and you'll learn to live freely and lightly (Matt. 11:28–30 MSG).
>
> Jesus

Missing What Really Matters

In verses 23–24 of Matthew 23, Jesus says:

> Woe to you, teachers of the law and Pharisees, you hypocrites! You give a tenth of your spices—mint, dill and cummin. But you have neglected the more important matters of the law—justice, mercy and faithfulness. You should have practiced the latter, without neglecting the former. You blind guides! You strain out a gnat but swallow a camel.

They made a big deal over the more detailed matters of the law—and in some cases rules that they had come up with on their own. But they were overlooking what was really important. Jesus gives the example of how the Pharisees handled tithing. The law required tithing of grain, wine, oil, and the firstborn of the flocks (Deut. 14:22–29). Leviticus 27:30 also mentions fruit from trees. But the Pharisees had greatly expanded this to include a tenth of even household spices. Jesus doesn't say this is wrong—but points out the problem that they are missing the big stuff, "justice, mercy and faithfulness" (v. 23).

If Jesus were preaching this sermon today, I think he might say something like:

> Woe to you, fans; if you would be as passionate about feeding the poor as you are your church's style of worship, then world hunger would end this week. Woe to you, fans; if you sacrificed as much to care for the homeless and hungry in the community as you do for your church building or place of worship, the need would be wiped out. Woe to you, fans; if you would be as zealous about caring for the sick as you are about a "Christmas tree" being called a "holiday tree," health insurance wouldn't be a problem.

We end up straining a gnat but not really paying any attention to the camel.

Maybe you grew up in a home where you were taught all about Jesus. Through fear and guilt you learned to keep as many of the rules as possible, hoping it would be enough to keep you out of hell. You were taught to observe different religious traditions and rituals in an effort to appease God. Instead of becoming a follower of Christ, you became a follower of religion.

It's not unusual for me to talk to Christian college-age kids who no longer go to church or see any need to. They have little if any interest in Jesus or anything spiritual, for that matter. Their parents, who raised them in the church, try and understand what went wrong.

A few months ago I was speaking in Houston, Texas, and a good-sized man, with a good-sized belt buckle, came up to me with tears in his eyes. He began to tell me the story of his prodigal daughter, how she went to college and totally turned her back on the faith. As soon as he started the story I knew how it would go. I've heard it so many times, even the details seem predictable. But when he finished, he didn't ask me why she was doing this or what had gone wrong. He wasn't looking for an explanation. Instead, with one sentence he put his finger on what he thought happened. Here's what he said,

We raised her in Church, but we didn't raise her in Christ.

Do you hear what he is saying? She was raised to look right on the outside but was not taught to give attention to the inside. Like some of you, she had been taught to keep all the rules and say the right prayers, but somehow missed that those things come from a personal and genuine relationship with Jesus. She was made to feel guilty for what she did wrong, but didn't realize God's amazing grace available through Christ.

not a fan story

Merrick Nunn

A few years ago I had everything any teenager could want; at least that's how it looked from the outside. My parents were together and successful. My dad is a lawyer, and my mom owns a business. We were always in church. I was a leader in every area and people looked up to me. I was good in sports, had all the right stuff, and the girls always liked me. I never had trouble imitating what it meant to be a good boy. When I was in seventh grade, though, I began to keep secrets about who I was becoming. That year, Satan got a hold of my life and wouldn't let go. I fell into a trap of pornography and lust and it became a driving desire of mine. I had girlfriend after girlfriend over the next few years, and usually she was the same as me, a great pretender. Honestly, I would treat her with respect in order to play the perfect boyfriend. It was all a masquerade. When I turned fifteen, I found out that my father was having an affair — one of many. I was in deep pain, but I only saw the hurt my father caused, more than the unconditional love my mother had shown. I became completely self-absorbed. Status and selfishness ruled my life. I used God to make me look good.

Because of the sexual sin in my life, I was becoming numb to how it was affecting my relationships. I was empty inside and searching for love in whatever way I could. I still went to church and believed that Jesus was Lord of my life, but I was being ruled by lust. I finally dated an amazing girl, who loved the Lord. Instead of surrendering my self-centeredness, I used her as my spiritual crutch. She made me feel better about my relationship with the Lord. When I was with her I was a good Christian, but when I wasn't, I was right back in a club somewhere, feeding the sin that was destroying me.

One day, while I was in the shower, I literally could feel the weight of all my sin on my back. I began to have vivid flashbacks of my life and all the people I had led down the wrong path. I began to see clearly how I had been two different people. I had been on mission trips and attended multiple youth retreats while in sexual sin at the same time. There were times I had proclaimed the Lord's name in the day and defied his authority at night. I was the false person, the deceiver. God allowed my eyes, in that moment, to be truly opened. I realized I was who he was talking about when he said, "Depart from me, I never knew you." God spoke so clearly to me, I could hear him saying to me, "Now or never, Merrick. Will you follow me?" I fell on my knees and wept in a way I never have before. I could barely talk, and when I finally did, all I could say was, "Yes."

I am Merrick Nunn and I am not a fan.

self-empowered
or spirit-filled?

John 16

For some who are fans, I know just the title of this chapter makes them a little nervous. When you read "Spirit-filled," you got a little bit uncomfortable. Fans tend to be comfortable talking about God and Jesus, but the third member is kind of like the Cousin Eddie of the Trinity; you just don't know what to do with him. It reminds me of how I'm treated by my in-laws. I married a girl from a small Kansas town.* She grew up on a farm several miles down a dirt road. In high school she raised pigs and drove a tractor. Her family tries to make me feel welcome, but whenever I show up I can almost hear that old *Sesame Street* song in the background, *One of these things is not like the others. One of these things just doesn't belong.*

The rest of the men show up for Thanksgiving wearing camo sprayed with deer urine, ready to go hunting after the big meal. I sit at the table in my designer shirt that is referred to as a "blouse" behind my back. I eat in silence as the men take turns telling about the deer they shot and the buck that got away.† About a half hour after lunch, I look around and realize that I'm the only grown man in the house. I walk into

---

* How small? Directions to her house include the following: "Turn right at the wagon wheel next to the dirt road." Eating out for special occasions requires a twenty-minute drive to Sonic for a foot-long. Tractors on the road outnumber cars. Livestock outnumber the people. "Swimming pool" means "stock tank."

† One year I told about the time I killed a deer, but apparently hitting one with my car doesn't count.

the kitchen, where the ladies are making pies, and ask, "Do you know where the men went?" My mother-in-law says, and I quote, "All the men are outside." Hello? Um ... clearly they're not all outside. Apparently they got on their four-wheelers and went to build a deer stand together, but no one thought to invite me. Now, I know they believe in my existence. I would even say that most of them like me. But they aren't sure what to do with me. I think that's how fans tend to approach the Holy Spirit. But the truth is you cannot be a follower unless you are filled with the Holy Spirit.

Fans who try to follow Jesus without this power will start to show signs. Sooner or later they will reach a point where they are frustrated by failures. You keep doing what you don't want to do and you don't do the things you really want to do. You promise others that you will change. "Things are going to be different this time," you say. And this time you really mean it. But the change rarely lasts more than a few days. You lie awake at night and promise yourself "Never again" ... never again will I lose my temper, never again will I lie to my parents, never again will I get on that website, never again will I go that far with my boyfriend or girlfriend. But soon you're lying awake at night staring at the ceiling and making the same promises. It just doesn't work. When we try to follow Jesus without being filled daily with the Spirit we find ourselves frustrated by our failures and exhausted by our efforts.

Recently my wife and I and our four kids flew into the Atlanta airport from the island of Hispaniola where we had spent a month on a mission trip. After landing, we grabbed our bags and began a long hike through the airport. When we travel my wife and I share the responsibilities. One of us packs lots of stuff and one of us carries it everywhere. That's how we've worked it out. So I'm carrying about a half dozen bags through the airport. They are just hanging all around me. It's just a moving pile of bags with my head sticking out of the top. We turn to go down a hallway that is about one hundred yards long. My wife and kids all get on a moving sidewalk, but I'm carrying a wide load and it's impossible for me to navigate the turn and I miss the on ramp. I wish you could have seen what it looked like from my perspective. They set the few bags they have on the moving sidewalk and just stand there watching me. I'm sweating like … well, like a man carrying a half dozen suitcases through the airport. I'm trying to keep up with the pace. We end up arriving at the end of the sidewalk at about the same time. But there's a difference. I'm frustrated, exhausted, and annoyed, and they are ready to keep moving. That's what our lives look like when we try the self-empowered hike, instead of the Spirit-filled walkway. Fans try to play the role of the Holy Spirit, but trying to be God has a tendency to wear you out. It will leave you tired and frustrated.

Fans trying to follow without being filled with the power of the Holy Spirit become overwhelmed by life's circumstances. They seem to be following Christ, but then something in life goes wrong and they don't have the power to overcome it. Instead of following Christ and sticking close to him in the storm they become discouraged and keep their distance.

Eventually something happens and you can't get through it on your own. Followers have discovered that it doesn't work without the power of the Spirit.

Diagnosing Fandom — ### QUESTION 5: Are You a Self-Empowered Fan or a Spirit-Filled Follower?

We've looked at a number of encounters in the Gospels where Jesus challenged people to define their relationship with him. He was intentionally separating the fans from the followers. For disciples this defining moment had to come when Jesus ascended into heaven leaving them here to advance his kingdom to the ends of the earth. If they were only fans of Jesus, one of two things would happen. They would go back to their old lives and resume their former careers. Show's over, it's time to go home. Or they would try to carry out this mission God gave them, but because they would depend on their own strength and efforts it would end in utter and complete failure and Jesus would disappear into human history. But in Acts 1, here's what Jesus said to his followers just before he ascended into heaven:

"You will receive power when the Holy Spirit comes on you; and you will be my witnesses in Jerusalem, and in all Judea and Samaria, and to the ends of the earth." After he said this, he was taken up before their very eyes, and a cloud hid him from their sight (Acts 1:8–9).

I'm sure this would have seemed overwhelming to his followers. It's one thing to follow Jesus when he's right there in the flesh leading the way. They could see him and talk to him. If they faced a storm, he was there to calm it. If they were hungry, he was there to provide food. If they were confused, he was there to help them understand. But as they watched him disappear into the clouds, they must have wondered how they could continue to follow him here on earth. They had no idea what to do next. They are uneducated. They are under resourced. They had no strategic plan. They had no special power. They had no political influence. How can they follow him if he isn't there to lead? But Jesus said to his followers, "You will receive power when the Holy Spirit comes on you." Fans may try to follow Jesus out of their own strength, but followers are empowered by the Holy Spirit.

Sometimes when we read through the Gospels we read the stories of the disciples following Jesus and we can't help but be a little envious. What would it have been like to follow Jesus in person? We're glad for the Holy Spirit, but we tend to think of him as being on the JV team of the Trinity. But that's not how Jesus portrayed the Holy Spirit to his followers. In John 16 we read one of the last conversations Jesus would have with his disciples before his arrest and crucifixion. He's trying to prepare them for his death, but they are in denial. They can't imagine losing Jesus as their leader, teacher, and friend. It's the worst possible news. But here's what Jesus says to them:

> But I tell you the truth: It is for your good that I am going away. Unless I go away, the Counselor will not come to you; but if I go, I will send him to you (John 16:7).

Did you catch that? Jesus, God in the flesh, says it's better for him to leave, because when he goes the Holy Spirit will come. It's better. Why would he say that? When I was in seminary I did a study of the references in the Bible that speak of God being *with* man. The Bible speaks of God being *with* Abraham. God was *with* Joseph. God was *with* Elisha. I noticed that most all of the references of "God being *with*" were in the Old Testament. It just wasn't in the New Testament. I couldn't figure out why that was. I kept thinking I was missing something. Here's what I discovered: there is a subtle but critical prepositional change from the Old Testament to the New Testament. In the Old Testament it says "God *with* us"—but in the New Testament it's "God *in* us" (emphasis mine). Jesus says, "It's better for you if I go"—because while God with you is good, God in you is better. Jesus could be *with* his followers; but the Holy Spirit would live *in* his followers.

Sometimes I hear people talk about the different men and women of the Old Testament, and there is a hint of jealousy. They may say it, or just insinuate it, but here's what they communicate ...

What would it have been like to hear God's voice and see him move in such powerful ways? I wish it was the same for us as it was for those whose stories we read about in Scripture. When I get to heaven I can't wait to ask David, Elijah, or Moses what it was like.

But I think it will be just the opposite in heaven. Before we can ask David what it was like to slay the giant, to win the battles, he'll say, *Tell me what it was like on earth to have the Holy Spirit living inside of you, giving you strength when you are weak.* We might say to Elijah, *What was it like to call down fire from heaven before the prophets of Baal and to raise that boy from the dead?* And I think Elijah might say, *Yeah, he actually ended up dying again. You tell me what it's like to have God living inside of you. What was it like to live life on earth with the Holy Spirit giving you joy when you're depressed or giving you the power to overcome that sin in your life?* We might say to Moses, *What was it like to follow the cloud by day and the fire by night? What was it like to meet with God on that mountain?* And Moses might say, *I had to climb that mountain to meet with God. You tell me what it was like to have him dwell within you every day. What was it like to have the Holy Spirit giving you directions when you didn't know what to do or where to go?*

In Acts chapter 1 Jesus promises his followers that they would receive power from the Holy Spirit, and the rest of Acts documents what God can do with Spirit-filled followers. In chapter 4 two of Jesus' closest followers, Peter and John, are brought before the spiritual leaders. And these guys can't figure out why these followers of Jesus are making such a difference. Peter and John didn't have the right theological training or religious credentials. The spiritual leaders are scratching their heads trying to figure out how such ordinary men are doing such extraordinary things. So they questioned them.

> They had Peter and John brought before them and began to question them: "By what power or what name did you do this?" (Acts 4:7).

It is clear to the religious leaders that Peter and John were not doing these things out of their own power. In the next verse Peter answers their question. But before we read what Peter says, here's what we're told in verse 8:

> Then Peter, filled with the Holy Spirit, said to them ...

After Peter speaks to them, verse 13 tells us the conclusion reached by these spiritual leaders:

> When they saw the courage of Peter and John and realized that they were unschooled, ordinary men, they were astonished ...

Filled with the power of the Spirit, these ordinary, unschooled followers of Jesus changed the world. In Romans 8:11 Paul illustrates just how powerful the Holy Spirit wants to be in our lives. He writes:

> The Spirit of God, who raised Jesus from the dead, lives in you (NLT).

The same Spirit that raised Christ from the dead now lives in his followers.

When you become a Christian you receive from God the gift of the Holy Spirit. That's his promise to all who put their faith in him. So it's not a question of whether or not you have access to this power of the Holy Spirit; the question is, have you accessed it? Fans may have received the gift of the Holy Spirit but they aren't being filled with the Holy Spirit.

This was a problem with the first-century church in Galatia. Paul had come in and preached a message of grace. People surrendered their lives to Christ and accepted his free gift. But soon after Paul headed out towards another city, a crew of false teachers known as the "Judaizers" came into the church and began pushing people back to the law. They began to put the emphasis on human effort and hard work rather than on the power of the Spirit. But here's how Paul addresses that:

> **Fans may have received the gift of the Holy Spirit but they aren't being filled with the Holy Spirit.**

> Are you so foolish? After beginning with the Spirit, are you now trying to attain your goal by human effort? (Gal. 3:3).

Paul points out that trying to live the Christian life out of your own power is ridiculous. Why would a person do that? Why would you walk when you can ride?

Weak Is Strong

Being filled with the power of the Spirit begins with an honest acknowledgment of our own weakness.

The truth is that most of us go to great lengths to disguise our weaknesses.

Some of you will be looking for jobs very soon. In fact, you may have already done mock interviews to help you prepare for future job interviews. Let me tell you the hardest question to answer in a job interview: "What's your greatest weakness?" How do you answer that? I'll tell what you don't do—you don't tell them the truth! Because if you do, they aren't going to hire you. You don't say, "I'm never on time. I compulsively make offensive noises. I constantly quote inappropriate lines from movies. I have trouble getting along with co-workers." You don't tell them those things, but you have to say something. What do you say?

Monster.com, the job search website, describes a variety of strategies for answering that question. One approach is to disguise your weakness as strength. For example, you might say, "I'm such a people person that sometimes my friendly disposition is too much positive energy for others." Or you say, "I work so hard that sometimes my life can be a little out of balance." Another strategy they recommend is to minimize your weakness by explaining how you've already overcome it: "I can be a very task-oriented person, but I've learned that working with people is the most effective way to accomplish a goal." A third strategy is to share a real weakness, but make sure it is completely irrelevant to the position. If you're applying to be a cashier you don't want to mention that you're not sure how to make change for a dollar. So you say something like, "Whenever I make ramen noodles I always overcook the noodles." Find a way around the question, but whatever you do, don't acknowledge your real weaknesses.

Can I make a small confession? Every once in a while when I'm at the gym I'll be using some weight equipment where you determine how much weight you'll be lifting by moving a stopper up and down on a set of weights. When I do the triceps pull I only use about forty pounds, which isn't very impressive. Part of the problem is that I don't think I have triceps. There's no actual evidence that they exist. But when I get up to leave, do you know what I do? I nonchalantly move the stopper from forty pounds to around seventy pounds so the next person will surely think to himself, *That guy's got some impressive triceps. He just humbly hides them under his baggy clothing.* That's what we do most of our lives—we try to reinforce this perception that we really are strong. That we've got our stuff together and we can handle anything that comes our way.

In Paul's Second letter to the Corinthians he spoke about how acknowledging our weakness makes room for Christ's power:

> I will boast all the more gladly about my weaknesses, so that Christ's power may rest on me. That is why, for Christ's sake, I delight in weaknesses ... For when I am weak, then I am strong (2 Cor. 12:9–10).

Paul understands that living in the power of the Spirit means shining a light on our weaknesses. This is what fans find so difficult. Most fans have learned to make sure everyone knows about their strengths, but that no one finds out about their weaknesses.

Paul reminds these followers in Galatia who had stopped living in the Spirit's power and had started to depend on themselves how foolish that is, and then he makes it clear what they need to do.

Since we live by the Spirit, let us keep in step with the Spirit (Gal. 5:25).

The picture is of someone walking, and every step they take, they take in the Spirit. You can't live by the Spirit if you *only acknowledge his presence one day a week* when you come to church.

Spiritual Breathing

The teaching of Bill Bright helped me learn to become a follower who is filled with the Spirit. He teaches a spiritual exercise called "Spiritual Breathing." The basic idea is that you live with a moment by moment awareness of the Spirit until walking in the Spirit becomes as natural —as habitual—as breathing. It's just part of who you are. Here's how it works: the moment you become aware of sin in your life you *exhale*. When you exhale, you breathe out and repent of your sin. Repentance becomes a natural response and clears out space in our hearts for the Spirit to fill us. So the moment you are prideful, jealous, lustful, harsh, selfish, dishonest, impatient, you *exhale* and repent of your sin.

The only way to be filled with the Spirit is to empty myself of me. When I empty me of me, it provides space for the Holy Spirit to fill me. Before you can be filled you must first be emptied. You can't hold up you glass to be filled if it's already full. When the Holy Spirit moves in and takes up residence, then you should constantly be moving yourself out. And, slowly, you find that your pride, your impatience, your selfishness, your lust, and whatever else is bottled inside you is carried out the door. Because if you are being filled with him there won't be as much room for you. So exhale and breathe out the clutter and darkness of you to make room to be filled with the Spirit.

And then you *inhale*. When you inhale you breathe in and pray to be filled with the Spirit and you surrender control over to him. For me, one of the most difficult parts of being filled is being still. It must be a family trait. A few years ago my youngest daughter was trying to catch one of about a half a dozen butterflies that were in the backyard. Her arms flailed as she darted around with urgent and frantic movements trying to seize one of these butterflies. I finally got her attention long enough to talk her into sitting still. And as she sat there in stillness and quietness, after a few moments a butterfly landed on her knee. For her, sitting quietly was much harder work than busily going after the butterflies. Sometimes it hard work to pray "fill me with your Spirit" and then be still, but the Holy Spirit is not caught, he is received.

Exhale. Inhale. As you practice this spiritual breathing it teaches you to keep in step with the Spirit. Followers live with a continual awareness of the Spirit's presence and a constant prayer to be filled with his power.

For fans, this will seem unnatural at first. You were not taught to keep in step with the Spirit. When you first began to walk as a toddler, it took complete concentration and lots of effort, but before long putting one foot in front of the other became completely natural. If you're a teenager and still find it takes all your concentration and willpower to walk, that's a sign there is something wrong. Likewise, the longer you practice keeping in step with the Spirit, the more natural it becomes. As you become more aware of his presence and pray daily for his power, what feels forced and unnatural now will become second nature. If it's not happening, you'll know something isn't right.

A surprising thing I've discovered over the years is that there are lots of churches like the one in Galatia. The message becomes "try harder," and the more people are around the church and the things of God, the more they slip into a "do-it-yourself" mentality. The emphasis is put more on their effort and self-discipline. Fans foolishly think that with enough hard work they can follow Jesus. People who grow up with that approach to faith will almost certainly walk away from it when they get older simply because they are too exhausted to keep trying.

As ridiculous as it seems to put our confidence in our own efforts, instead of the Holy Spirit's power, I can easily find myself trying to operate that way. This was especially true for me early on in ministry. Instead of admitting my weakness and declaring my complete dependence on God, I tried to do it myself.

When we moved into our current house, I saved the heaviest piece of furniture for last. It was the desk from my office. I tried to slide it, but the legs kept getting caught. Eventually I figured out that if I flipped it over so the top was on the floor and the feet were up in the air I could slide it across the carpet. I was pushing with everything I had and was slowly making progress. About that time my four-year-old son came over and asked if he could help me. He stood between my arms and began to push. Together we started sliding it across the floor. He was pushing and grunting as we inched our way along. Then he stopped, looked up at me, and said, "Dad, you're in my way." I could easily push it just fine by myself. He couldn't budge it, but insisted on doing it himself. He thought he was pushing the desk. I couldn't help but laugh.

When I started a new church in Los Angeles County, California, I found that I was overwhelmed with pressure and stress. I was working more than seventy hours a week. My wife would ask me to take a day off and I would say, "I can't." I wasn't sleeping well at night. When the church was about a year old I woke up in the night and I had this strange sense that God was laughing at me. I know that seems strange, and perhaps it was the sleeping pills, but it was a very real moment that I remember well. I laid there trying to discern what it was about. Why was God laughing at me? I never could quite figure it out, but had often wondered what it meant. And then about five years later, when my son and I were pushing a desk across the floor and he looked up and said, "Dad, you're in my way," I understood. The moment I started laughing at my son's comment, that dream came back to my mind. And I realized why God was laughing at me. I thought I was pushing the desk. I know that's ridiculous, but instead of recognizing God's power and strength I started to think it all depended on me.

Fans eventually get burned out from trying to live the Christian life out of their own efforts. If you are depending on your own strength to follow Christ, you will soon find yourself drained and defeated. Jesus promised his followers that the Spirit would come on them in power.

Followers of Jesus understand that it's a journey they were never to make alone. Instead we keep in step with the Spirit and he supernaturally gives us the strength and the power we need.

One of the challenges in talking about followers being filled with the Holy Spirit is that being filled with the Holy Spirit is often thought of and talked about in a very ethereal way while following Jesus seems to be more physical. I wanted to find a way to better explain or illustrate what it looks like when these things come together and a follower is filled with the Holy Spirit. I asked my Facebook friends to finish this sentence for me, **"By the power of the Holy Spirit ..."** Within twenty-four hours I had over one hundred responses:

I finally forgave my dad for walking out.

I talked to my roommate about my faith.

I lost 150 pounds.

I'm raising a baby as teen mom.

I have forgiven my mom for her cheating on my dad.

I have two brothers my parents adopted from Ethiopia.

I overcame drug addiction.

I stopped looking at porn.

I overcame a shopping addiction.

I overcame an eating disorder.

I am no longer cutting myself.

I returned something I stole.

I walked away from a boyfriend and a relationship that I knew God didn't want.

My brother returned home after we hadn't heard from him for three years.

I got through a tough time when my best friend died in a car accident.

Story after story from followers who are filled with the Holy Spirit. Fans have a hard time telling stories like that. What's your story?

not a fan story

Summer Rines

It was really hard to follow Jesus when I didn't love myself. For years, I have struggled with an eating disorder, and I know now it's something I will always struggle with. And although I have made considerable progress, there are still times when I struggle. What I am discovering is that those are the times that I am ignoring God's voice in my life and following something or someone other than Jesus.

Looking back on my journey, I can see that I was trying to handle this sickness on my own. And because I tried to be the one in control, I was not only damaging my own life, but the lives of those around me. I was only able to worship and love Jesus as long as I was at peace with my body. But when push came to shove, I wasn't willing to set aside my selfishness and vanity. I wasn't willing to love and serve everyone, including God, in spite of my own struggles. A follower of Jesus dies to every disease and insecurity, no matter how hard and scary it is, and allows him to take control. For the longest time I couldn't bring myself to give the controls of this area of my life over to him.

Finally I surrendered everything to him. When I was baptized and lowered into the water, I was consciously giving up a lot of things. I was trying to let go of a lot of stuff, including control over my disease. Honestly, it hasn't been easy. Dying completely to this disease has been the biggest struggle in my walk with Christ. But it's different now. Before I had tried and tried to find victory, but now instead of just trying, I am trusting the power of the Holy Spirit in my life. Each day starts with denying myself, surrendering to him, and living in the power of the Holy Spirit. That's how I started today and it is how I will start tomorrow. My name is Summer Rines, and I am not a fan.

the relationship defined

Matthew 7

I began the first chapter with a simple question: "Are you a follower of Jesus?" We have looked at a number of encounters that Jesus had with people during his time on earth. These were defining moments for each of them as it was revealed if they were fans or followers. After studying some of these encounters in Scripture, maybe you've decided that you need to take a closer look at where you stand with Jesus. I want you to know it has not been my objective to cause true followers of Christ to doubt or question their standing with God. It's my hope that as we looked at what separates fans from followers that you have been affirmed in your faith and confirmed in your commitment as a follower. But I know there are many of you who have called yourselves Christians (by definition Christ-followers), but as you have honestly defined what you have with Jesus, it has become clear that you aren't following Christ.

My prayer is that your eyes would be opened and the Spirit would awaken your soul to the kind of relationship Christ desires to have with you. I am jealous for you to discover that now and not waste another day living with some sort of watered-down and diluted form of Christianity. I want you to experience this, not just so you can experience the life-giving, soul-satisfying existence on this planet that God wants you to have, but because I believe eternity hangs in the balance. Bottom line is this ... there will be a day when we stand before God, and on that day many who thought themselves followers will be identified as nothing more than fans. I am not speculating or predicting; Jesus has already spoken clearly about this in Matthew 7.

Though I believe in the assurance of our salvation, I also believe that we are to work out our salvation with fear and trembling (Phil. 2:12). When it comes to where we will spend eternity we can't be afraid to ask the hard questions and take an honest look at the answers that our lives offer. Is it possible that when asked, "Are you a follower of Jesus?" you quickly responded, "Yes," but one day you will be exposed as nothing more than a fan?

Not long ago I was returning to Louisville from a quick trip to Cincinnati. There is a highway between Cincinnati and Louisville called I–71. It's a straight shot and takes about an hour. I was heading home in plenty of time to have dinner with my family. The radio was turned up, it was a beautiful day, and I was enjoying the journey. After about an hour I knew I was getting close to Louisville, but then I saw a sign that said, "Welcome to Lexington."

There is a place right outside Cincinnati where, if you're not real careful, you can easily miss where I–71 towards Louisville splits off from I–75 towards Lexington. This is a frequent mistake and has happened to a lot of people making this trip. For close to an hour I was completely convinced I was on I–71, but all along I was on I–75. It never occurred to me that I was going the wrong way. The road I was on felt right to me. I'm sure there were signs and markers along the way indicating that I was on I–75, but they never got my attention. It never occurred to me that I might be going the wrong way. I had the radio turned up, and I was singing along to the music, completely oblivious. I never allowed for the possibility that I was on the wrong road.

In Matthew chapter 7 Jesus talks about two different roads that lead to different places:

> Enter through the narrow gate. For wide is the gate and broad is the road that leads to destruction, and many enter through it. But small is the gate and narrow the road that leads to life, and only a few find it (Matt. 7:13–14).

Many people take the wrong road and only few find the narrow path. If that is true, then wouldn't it make sense for us to slow down? Shouldn't we hit the brakes, pull over to the side, and make sure that we are on the road that leads to life? This teaching of Jesus is the conclusion of his sermon known as "The Sermon on the Mount." It's a sermon that has been all about raising the bar of the commitment for those who would follow him. It's a narrow road, but it's a road that leads to life.

I'm just wondering, is it possible that you think you are on the narrow road but you are actually on the broad road? Could it be that you have set cruise control, turned up the Christian radio, and are traveling down the road of destruction?

Donald Whitney once said, "If a person is wrong about being right with God, then ultimately it really doesn't matter what he or she is right about." So before you continue driving down the road, I'm just asking you to slow down the car and look at some of the signs and ask yourself what road you are on. Is it possible that you are wrong about being right with God? Jesus continues his teaching in Matthew 7:

> Not everyone who says to me, "Lord, Lord" will enter the kingdom of heaven, but only the one who does the will of my Father who is in heaven. Many will say to me on that day, "Lord, Lord, did we not prophesy in your name and in your name drive out demons and in your name perform many miracles?" Then I will tell them plainly, "I never knew you. Away from me, you evildoers!"
>
> Matthew 7:21–23

It wouldn't surprise me if Jesus said a *few* will stand before God on Judgment Day convinced that everything is fine only to find out otherwise. But he doesn't say *few*. He doesn't say *some*. He says "many." Many who assumed they were on the path to heaven will find out that heaven is not their destination.

So if you've pulled the car over to the side of the road I want you to ask yourself a couple of important questions from what Jesus teaches in Matthew 7.

QUESTION 1: Does Your Life Reflect What You Say You Believe?

In verse 21 we read, "Not everyone who says ... but only he who does ..." Jesus makes a distinction between fans and followers by contrasting the word "says" with the word "does." We live at a time when we have become increasingly comfortable with separating what we say we believe with how we live. We have convinced ourselves that our beliefs are sincere even if they have no impact on how we live. Let me give you a few examples of this mentality.

If I did a survey and asked Americans, "Do you believe it's important to eat right and exercise?" most all of them would say, "Yes, I believe that." Americans overwhelmingly say their health is important. But the most popular food at state fairs is a bacon cheeseburger with a bun made out of two Krispy Kreme donuts. You're charged extra if you want chocolate-covered bacon.* Here's another example: When you were growing up your dad might have said to people something like, "I believe in the importance of family. Nothing is more important to me than my family." But he never made it to your recitals or your games. He was consumed with work and always on his phone. And he may have said, "I believe family matters most," but his actions revealed a different belief.

We are saved by God's grace when we believe in Jesus and put our faith in him, but biblical belief is more than something we confess with our mouths; it's something we confess with our lives.

So a fan may say "Lord, Lord," but a fan doesn't live "Lord, Lord." You say, "I am a follower." I hear you, but when is the last time you fed the hungry, clothed the naked, visited the prisoner? You say, "I am a follower." Well that's great, but what do you do when you get in an argument with your parents? I want to know if you're the one who reaches over and says to your mom or dad, "I'm sorry. I was wrong." What do you do when a friend starts to gossip about a classmate? What do you do when the movie you're watching continues to take God's name in vain? A belief is more than what we say.

---

* Worth every penny in my opinion. Logically speaking, if you're going to eat a donut bacon cheeseburger, you might as well put some chocolate on your bacon.

Imagine that you and I are neighbors and my family goes on a mission trip together for a month. I ask if you would mind watching the house while we are gone. That sounds like easy money so you agree. Let's imagine that before we leave I give you a notebook with ten or twelve pages of fairly detailed instructions for taking care of the house and the pets. I tell you when to water the plants. I write out where to find the food for the cat and how much food to give it. I remind you to get the mail. I explain the trash day is early on Thursday morning. I tell you if you use the restroom in the house not to use the downstairs toilet because it overflows. You look through the notebook and commit to doing what it says. Now I want you to imagine I come back and all the plants are dead. The garage is full of trash. The toilet has been overflowing for days and the basement is flooded. Then I look in the backyard and there is a little gravesite where the cat has been buried. I go over to your house but before I have a chance to lay into you, you start explaining how helpful the notebook was. In fact you say that you had memorized certain sections and you show me where different areas of the notebook have been highlighted. You tell me that you read different parts of it every night before going to bed. What am I going to say? I'm going to say, "Away from me, you evildoer!" Why? Well, you may have spoken words of commitment, but there is no evidence that those words meant anything.

The book of James in the Bible addresses this. James wants his readers to understand biblical belief:

> What good is it, my brothers, if a man claims to have faith but has no deeds? Can such faith save him? Suppose a brother or sister is without clothes and daily food. If one of you says to him, "Go, I wish you well; keep warm and well fed," but does nothing about his physical needs, what good is it? (James 2:14–16).

More Than a Feeling

Here's what fans tend to do: they confuse their feelings for faith. But your feelings aren't faith until they are expressed. This hit me in a very personal way a number of years ago. I was up late at night flipping through the channels and I came across a program showing images of children with bloated stomachs who were malnourished and starving. I laid there on my couch watching these heart-wrenching images. My eyes welled up with tears. My heart broke for those children. I was really moved. After a few minutes I got up from the couch, feeling pretty good about myself as a Christian; after all, not everyone would have such a sensitive heart towards the hurting. I felt something, but did nothing, and that's not biblical belief. That's just one example. But faith is more than a feeling. As we see in Hebrews 11, faith should have a story attached to it. There is a tendency to define yourself as a follower based on how you feel about Jesus, but following requires there to be more than a feeling. Following requires movement.

James concludes in verse 17:

> Faith by itself, if it is not accompanied by action, is dead.

When I was studying about the word "belief" I came across a secular article written by a psychiatrist. In the article he addressed the beliefs of his patients that had no basis in reality. A patient may sincerely believe he could fly—but that didn't mean anything because there was nothing to back that up. The patient might be an abusive husband who sincerely believes abuse is wrong—but he doesn't really believe that because his stated belief is contradicted by reality. But when the psychiatrist was speaking about his patients with beliefs that had no basis in reality he didn't call them "beliefs." Do you know what he called them? He called them "delusions." We don't often think of it this way, but here's an important truth that needs some attention in circles of faith: A belief, no matter how sincere, if not reflected in reality isn't a belief; it's a delusion.

A belief, no matter how sincere, if not reflected in reality isn't a belief; it's a delusion.

QUESTION 2: Do You Think You're on the Right Road Because of What You've Done?

Just as dangerous as assuming that what we say alone shows that we are on the right road is the assumption that what we do alone moves us down the narrow road. Notice the ways the fans defend themselves in Matthew 7. They will say to Jesus on that day, "We prophesied, we drove out demons, we performed miracles." Their confidence is in their righteous acts and their good deeds. One of the ways you know you're more fan than follower is that when I asked, "Are you a follower?" your mind immediately went to the fact that you go to church, put some money in the plate, and volunteer from time to time.

The hypothetical examples of righteousness that Jesus chooses in Matthew 7 are somewhat surprising. They seem pretty impressive from where I sit. I've never driven out demons or performed miracles. If they can't get in with their list, there's no way my list is going to get me into heaven. And I think that's exactly the point Jesus is trying to make. It seems that Jesus intentionally chooses the more dramatic and extraordinary spiritual achievements to make one thing clear: No matter how much good you do, no matter what you accomplish for the kingdom, that's not what makes you a true follower.

Ultimately the question that will identify you as a fan or follower isn't what you say or what you do. Those things matter, but only to the extent that they reflect the answer to this last question.

QUESTION 3: Do I Know Jesus and Does He Know Me?

That's what it comes down to in Matthew 7. That's the dividing line that Jesus identifies. In verse 23 he says to the fans, "I never knew you." So it comes down to a personal relationship with Jesus where you know him and are known by him. We want to put the emphasis on what we say and do. Those things are more measurable. They are tangible. We can point to them in the courtroom as evidence. But Jesus identifies his true followers based upon an intimate relationship. What we say and what we do overflows out of the relationship we have with him.

Next time you go out to eat I have a challenge for you. Look around the restaurant and identify the couples. Once the couples have been located, pay attention to how they talk to each other and try to guess what their relationship status is. Don't eavesdrop. Part of the challenge is to guess the relationship without hearing the conversations. My wife and I were recently on date and we played this little game. There were two couples at different tables. At the first table was a young couple clearly in love. They may have been newlyweds, but my guess is they were still dating. They were sitting on the same side of the booth, snuggled up, talking nonstop, laughing at each other's jokes. Their food was getting cold. They didn't care. Next to them was this elderly couple, and I'm guessing they had been married for decades. They did not say a word. Nothing. I watched as they just sat there in silence, not saying anything. I said to my wife, "Isn't that kind of sad? It starts off this way, with this couple just talking, talking, talking, so much to say, so much to share, and then decades later you have this elderly couple just sitting there in silence. It's sad." And my wife said, "I think it's kind of sweet."

I kind of nodded my head in silence, trying to be agreeable, but I was horribly confused. Then it hit me, or at least I think it did. It's sweet because they didn't *have* to say anything. Being together, focused on one another, even in silence, was a picture of the kind of relationship she wanted. If you asked me, I would have pointed to the fact that I took her out on a date to a nice restaurant as evidence that I am a good husband, but as far as she's concerned that doesn't mean much if she doesn't have my attention. If I'm watching the TV behind her instead of paying attention to her, she doesn't even qualify it as a date. We could go to the nicest restaurant in town and I could give her an expensive gift, but none of that will mean anything if she doesn't feel like I just want to be with her, know her, and let her know me. More than my words, more than my thoughtful acts, she wants my heart. She wants to know me.

Really, that is an indicator of God's love for us. More than he wants our acts of piety, more than he wants our adherence to religion, more than he wants our observance of rules and rituals, more than he wants our words of affection, he simply wants to know us and for us to know him. And ultimately that's how our relationship with him will be defined. And if that isn't there, all the prophesying, exorcisms, and miracles in the world won't matter.

Awhile back, I was sitting down with an upset father and his estranged daughter. They had not seen eye to eye since she was fifteen, and they were trying one last time, before she graduated, to get on the same page. I sat and listened as they fought back and forth with each other. She accused him of being preoccupied, uncaring but at the same time overprotective. He was defensive and rattled off a list of things he had done for her. "What else could I do?! I work hard to make sure all your needs are met. Without you even asking I went and surprised you with a new car for your sixteenth birthday!" He then starts to compare himself to other fathers. "What other dads to you know that give their daughters a credit card? What other dads are sending their kids to a top school?" He then closes with a dramatic, "What more do you want from me?"

She is silent. She looks off to the side and faces away from her daddy. She looks down and fidgets with an invisible spot on her jeans. She opens her eyes but continues to face the wall. Then she says, "I just don't feel like we even know each other."

In the end, that's really what mattered.

Just slow down for a moment and ask yourself: *Does Jesus know me?* Because a day is coming where many who have said the right things and done the right things will hear Jesus say, *"Away from me. I never knew you."*

Again, please understand, I'm not trying to make you paranoid. I believe what the Bible teaches about salvation. I believe that we are saved by the grace of God through faith in Jesus Christ (Eph. 2:8). I believe it is God alone who is able to keep us from falling (Jude 1:24). I believe that nothing can separate us from the love of God (Rom. 8:38–39). But I also believe the Bible clearly teaches that there will be those who think they are saved but who are not. They will live out their lives with a false assurance of salvation. They will think of themselves as followers, but a day will come when they'll be pronounced as nothing more than fans.

After I first preached this "Not a Fan" message I had an experience with a new member of our church that convinced me the whole church needed to hear this message. It began when a young single father started coming to church. He had grown up in the church and made a decision for Jesus as a kid but had never really committed to him. But within a few months of coming to church he was all-in. He fell in love with Jesus. He had discovered the pearl of great price and it was worth everything he had. The change in his life was pretty dramatic. His relationship with Jesus turned his life upside down. Before following Jesus, his life consisted, in his words, of "going out, drinking, smoking pot, and chasing girls." He'd show up to work with a hangover more often than not. He was full of anger and didn't know why. He felt like he was running in circles with no purpose, just going through life aimlessly. But following Jesus brought a radical change to his life. You spend a few minutes with him and it's easy to see the joy that he has found in Christ. He is constantly at church, serving in whatever way he can. He's a single dad with plenty of financial struggles, but when he became a Christian he decided that he would no longer work during church times, even though he needed the hours. He started to give generously even though things were tight.

Not long ago he asked if I would have coffee sometime with him and his mom. I did not know his mom but I said I would meet with them. When the three of us sat down for coffee I thought I knew what she wanted to talk to me about. I was aware that she went to a different church in town and I assumed that she wanted to meet with me to say thank you. I thought she wanted to express appreciation for what was happening in her son's life. But that wasn't the case. She was upset with him. She blamed me and she blamed the church, because she said, "My son has taken all of this too far." She was not pleased with how much time he was spending at the church. Some of the relatives were bothered by his desire to always want to pray before the family meals. He wouldn't be quiet about the sermons and was handing out CDs of the messages. She didn't think it was wise for him to give some of his hard earned money to the church. And lately he had been talking about going on a mission trip. After she made her case that he had taken this all too far, with a tone of frustration she asked me, "Can you please tell him that the Bible teaches 'everything in moderation'? Can you please tell him that it doesn't have to be all or nothing?"

I tried to keep a pleasant smile, but my teeth were clenched, and my breath was short. I was feeling defensive of my friend. I could feel my eyebrows narrowing and saw my nostrils flare. So I did what I always do when I get angry; I started quoting Scripture from Revelation. I said to this lady who had been in church most of her life, "In Revelation 3 Jesus says to the Christians in Laodicea, 'You are neither hot or cold but because you are lukewarm—I'm about to spit you out of my mouth.' Jesus doesn't say, 'Everything in moderation'; he says you can't be my follower if you don't give up everything. His invitation is an all or nothing invitation."

Jesus has defined the relationship he wants with you. He is not interested in enthusiastic admirers who practice everything in moderation and don't get carried away. He wants completely committed followers.

part 2

an invitation
to follow
(the unedited version)

anyone —
an open invitation

The journey from fan to follower begins by identifying the fan within us. To help us do that we have stepped into the scenes of different encounters Jesus had with people during his time on earth. Inevitably Jesus would put them in a position where they had to define their relationship with him. Was it casual or committed? Many of them were exposed to be nothing more than fans, just enthusiastic admirers of Jesus at best. It's not that fans don't want a relationship with Jesus; it's that they want the relationship with him on their terms. The real question we must ask is this: What kind of relationship does Jesus want to have with us? That's what matters. What are his terms? What would he say it really means to follow him?

Chances are, if you have one verse of the Bible memorized it would be John 3:16. It's a great verse that tells us a beautiful truth. Quick, can you say it without looking? I'll make it fill-in-the-blank to help you out.

For God so _____ the _____ that he gave his only _____, that whosoever _____ in him will not perish but have _____ life.

There is a reason why that is the most often quoted verse of the Bible.* In that one verse we read that God loves us, Jesus died for us, and that we can have eternal life through him. It's not unusual to go to a sporting event of some kind and see someone holding up a sign that

---

* One survey showed the most memorized verse in the Bible was "God helps those who help themselves." Umm ... that was Benjamin Franklin.

says "JOHN 3:16."* But I've never seen someone hold up a sign that says "LUKE 9:23." Quick, say that one without looking. That may be a little tougher. But Luke 9:23 also records the words of Jesus. In fact, unlike John 3:16, these words of Jesus in Luke 9:23 are recorded in three of the four Gospels. Here they are:

> If anyone would come after me, he must deny himself and take up his cross daily and follow me.

Now do you understand why no one paints that on a board and holds it up at a game? It doesn't seem like a very appealing advertisement for Christianity. Verses like that one can make it difficult to recruit new Christians. But the truth is that John 3:16 and Luke 9:23 have to go together in order for there to be an accurate understanding of the gospel's invitation.

John 3:16 emphasizes *believing*.

Luke 9:23 focuses on *following*.

Those two things must necessarily go together. There is no believing without following. There is no John 3:16 without Luke 9:23.

In the first section we identified where things stand in our relationship with Jesus. In this section we will discover where he wants to take us when we decide to follow him. These next few chapters will examine the invitation of Jesus to follow him from Luke 9:23. In this passage Jesus clearly lays out his expectations of his followers. This verse defines the relationship Jesus wants to have. It spells out his terms so that we can know exactly what we are agreeing to when we make a decision to follow.

Anyone Means Everyone

Jesus begins his call to follow him with these two words, *If anyone ...*

Anyone is a significant word because it makes it clear whom he is inviting. He is inviting *anyone. Anyone* is an all-inclusive word. *Anyone*

---

* My favorite sign held up at a game read, "The guy behind me can't see."

means *everyone*. Jesus doesn't begin with a list of pre-qualifications. His invitation to follow is addressed to *Anyone*. Many people don't realize they've been invited to follow. They think, "Not after what I've done. He wouldn't want me to follow him. I would never make the cut." They assume they aren't qualified and as a result never take seriously what it means to follow Jesus. After all, what's the point of auditioning for the part or trying out for the team if you know you don't have a shot?

■

A few years ago, my wife bought a white love seat to go in the room with the white carpet in our house. I should tell you we didn't put in the white carpet; it was the lovely decision of the childless couple that occupied the residence prior to us. My wife justified buying the white love seat because it was so cheap that it would have been poor stewardship not to buy it. So we had a white couch on white carpet. Maybe your parents had a room like this at home. A room that is only used by certain people on special occasions. As a result, my wife laid down the law and made sure that the kids knew they were not allowed in the "White Room." It seemed to be working fine, until one day my wife was straightening up in that room and discovered a secret that someone had been keeping. She happened to flip over one of the couch cushions and there was a stain. She called me into the room and showed me the pink fingernail polish blotched on the white cushion. She wasn't happy. We called our girls into the room. She had the cushion flipped back over so you couldn't see the stain. The interrogation was about to begin, but as I reached toward the cushion to expose the stain, my middle daughter Morgan cracked. Like many of us would, she turned and ran up the steps.

■

Most of us are hiding some stains. Our worst fear is that someone will flip the cushion over and discover what we've tried to hide. But because Jesus knows about our stains we think that disqualifies us. Surely our stains get our names scratched off the invitation list to be a follower of Christ. He wouldn't want us.

If any of his closest followers felt that way it had to be Matthew. When we are first introduced to Matthew he had stopped trying long ago to hide his stains. They were significant enough that it's highly probable that his family and friends had written him off. At the very least, he was a massive disappointment to his parents. They had much different plans for their son. We know this because Matthew has another name: Levi. To be given that name meant that your parents expected you to serve the Lord as the Levites of the Old Testament did. From birth, he was set aside to be a spiritual leader for the nation of Israel. Matthew's father, grandfather, and great-grandfather were likely all priests who served the Lord. By age twelve, Matthew would have had the first five books of the Bible memorized. It's likely that Matthew tried to become a disciple of one of the rabbis. But if he sent in his application, it was turned down. He didn't make the cut. Matthew had flunked out of rabbi school. He couldn't measure up.

Whatever happened, we know that something had definitely gone wrong. Instead of serving the Lord, he decided to serve himself. He turned his back on his own people and became a tax collector for the Romans. Essentially his job description was to unfairly take money from his people and give it to the occupying Roman government. Even if he'd collected taxes fairly, he was working for the enemy. But in those days there was no such thing as an honest tax collector. They would cheat the people to line their own pockets. A tax collector was seen as a religious and social outcast. He was ceremonially unclean; he wasn't even allowed into the outer court of the tabernacle. His name had been scratched off the membership.

And you and me, we have a lot in common with Matthew. Maybe you're not stealing money from your neighbors, but we've all become disappointments. We haven't measured up; we haven't made the cut. The Bible says in Romans that all of us have sinned and fallen short of the glory of God. We've said things we shouldn't have said. We've done things we wish we wouldn't have done. And as hard as we have scrubbed the stain, it just won't come out.

I can't help but wonder if in an attempt to ignore the stains in his life Matthew had chosen the life of a tax collector. That can happen with poor choices, right? One mistake snowballs into the next and eventually you think, *"What's the point? Why even try anymore?"* Whatever Matthew's past, he had reached a point where he was no longer even trying to hide it.

Every day Matthew sat at his tax collector booth on a busy street. As a boy growing up he never imagined it would come to this. In moments where he was honest with himself, maybe late at night staring up at the ceiling, he had to be full of guilt and regret. If only he could start over and do things differently. But what could he do now? His stains were set. They were never coming out.

■

Just before I flipped over the cushion, Morgan turned and ran. She headed up the steps and hid. I went after her. I called her name a few times. She didn't answer. I began to check the rooms and eventually found her in her closet with her head buried in her knees. I could hear her crying. She didn't want to look up. I got down in the closet with her and put my hand on her back. I wondered what she thought my response was going to be. Did she think I would get angry? Did she think I would yell? Was she afraid that I wouldn't love her? We went downstairs together and she told her mom and me what happened. She let out the secret she had been keeping for months. She had spilled the fingernail polish, and then she tried to clean it up. She scrubbed and scrubbed, but the stain just got worse.

Eventually, she flipped the cushion over to hide what she had done. She said she had felt sick to her stomach every time we were in that room. She was scared that we would find out. And then she asked a question that melted us. She looked up with her big brown eyes full of tears and asked, "Do you still love me?"

■

My guess is Matthew no longer asked that question. He couldn't imagine that God still wanted him. I'm sure Matthew had heard about a new rabbi on the scene. His name was Jesus and he was doing things differently. And then one day, Matthew is at his tax collector's booth and Jesus stops by and speaks to him. No one would have predicted what Jesus would say. It was only two words, but these two words changed everything for Matthew. Jesus said, "Follow me." A Jewish rabbi asking a tax collector for the Roman oppressors to be one of his followers? It's hard to overstate how unthinkable that scenario would have been for those close by.

It's important to understand what it meant in that culture for Jesus to be a rabbi. He may have been a homeless, unconventional rabbi, but he was a rabbi nonetheless. And a rabbi was a teacher of God's Word, which, at the time, was the Old Testament. Rabbis had extensive knowledge of the Torah (the first five books of the Bible) and all of the writings of the prophets.

Rabbis were also special because they had a group of Talmidim (pronounced *tal-mee-deem*). The word *Talmid* translates to "disciple" or "student." So, essentially, every rabbi had a class of students, and this was an incredibly exclusive group. Most people didn't end up as students of rabbis. Those who didn't make the cut most often ended up learning some sort of trade, typically one that was passed down in their family.

For those students wanting to become the Talmid of a particular rabbi, there was an application process. There were hefty pre-requisites before even being considered. These were the equivalent of the GPA and transcript pre-requisites for getting into an elite college or academy. If you want to go to Harvard, you better have a 4.0 GPA, or a 36 on your ACT, or a 2400 SAT score. Without those kinds of stats, you're probably not going to cut it. The same goes for a Talmid applying to join a rabbi's school.

Talmidim had to have an impressive knowledge of Scripture, and a rabbi would quiz prospective Talmid, asking them to recite an entire book. Or they might ask a question like, *"What is the number of times the name of the Lord was used in the eleventh chapter of Leviticus?"* The selection was an intense, painstaking process. But rabbis had to be thorough, because the excellence of the student reflected the excellence of the teacher. The teacher was known for his students. If a rabbi just let in anyone, it would be clear that he was not a sought-after teacher. On the other hand, if a rabbi's group of Talmidim were an especially brilliant and elite group, the rabbi would be respected and admired.

So the rabbis would take applications for followers. But that's not the way rabbi Jesus went about getting followers. Instead of followers applying, Jesus invited followers. This approach of going to someone and inviting him just wasn't done. A rabbi wouldn't humble himself, or extend himself in that way. A rabbi wouldn't risk rejection; a rabbi would do the rejecting. But Jesus takes the initiative. It would have been shocking enough if he had simply allowed Matthew to follow him, but Jesus actually extends the invitation. He says to Matthew, "Follow me."

Anyone hearing this exchange would have been shocked. I'm sure the other disciples would have been offended. *A tax collector?* He's not only a sinner; he sins for a living. Jesus finds Matthew hiding behind this tax collector's booth, and when Jesus comes by Matthew expects a pointed finger and words of rejection. Instead he finds open arms and a gracious invitation.

■

Morgan asked, "Do you still love me?" My wife knelt down beside her on the floor, and she whispered to our daughter, *"Morgan, you could never make a big enough stain to keep me from loving you."* I wish I could tell you that somehow we were able to get the stain out and make the couch white again ... but that stain is still there. It will always be there. But a funny thing happened. Morgan started telling the story of the stained white couch. She likes to show people the stain and tell them what happened. Why? Because a stain that once represented shame and guilt and fear of rejection now represents love, grace, and acceptance.

■

Do you know how we know about Matthew's past as a tax collector? Do you know how we know that his friends were prostitutes, drunkards, and thieves? The reason we know all of that is because Matthew tells us. He calls us into the living room and shows us the stain on a couch and tells us the story of love and grace.

When Jesus invited Matthew to follow, he was making it clear that this is an invitation extended not solely to the religious elite, the morally upright, and those who have their lives together. But it is an invitation to all of us who are hiding some stains. Jesus throws out the ivy-league application process and gives an open invitation.

Have you ever seen one of those car dealership commercials that advertises, "Anyone can buy a car here!" But if you look closely there is an asterisk next to that statement. At the bottom of the screen there is an asterisk with three letters: "W. A. C." You know what W. A. C. stands for? "With Approved Credit."

That's what they mean by *Anyone.*

Anyone who meets the qualifications.

Anyone who makes it through the approval process.

When we read the word *anyone* in the invitation of Jesus we can't help but think there must be an asterisk next to it. Even if there wasn't one when Jesus spoke these words, it seems that over the years the church has put an asterisk next to his invitation. The sign out front of the church says, *We Welcome Anyone and Everyone.* But if you look real close you'll find an asterisk. And it turns out that *Anyone* means people who appear to have their lives together and don't have visible struggles. *Anyone* does not include those who struggle with addictions. *Anyone* does not mean people with tattoos or piercings. *Anyone* means people who dress appropriately. *Anyone* means those from certain social and economic backgrounds. *Anyone* may mean those who are affiliated with a certain political party. *Anyone* means people who have a certain taste in music.

When I was living in California, I had quite a few friends that lived in what were called "gated communities." To get into their neighborhoods you had to pass through a guarded gate. On one occasion I went to visit a friend of mine and the guard stopped me. He was reluctant to let me in. I hadn't shaved in a few days and I was wearing a baseball cap. Not only that, I had a nasty bruise on my face where I had been shot playing paintball a few days earlier. I was driving a beat-up Plymouth Breeze. Due to an unfortunate accident with a mailbox, that was so not my fault, the side mirror of my car was duct-taped on. When I had first pulled up to the gate I probably had my music up a little loud. The guard was not happy to see me. He did not say, "Welcome! Come right in!" He did not greet me with a warm embrace. I told him I was there at the invitation of a friend in the neighborhood. He was skeptical. He wanted to know my name, where I lived, and how I knew the person who had invited me. He took my driver's license and examined it as if it might be laced with explosives. Eventually he called my friend, who confirmed the invitation, and he let me in. But it wasn't because he wanted to. He clearly did not approve of me being there.

That happens sometimes in our church communities. We say anyone can follow, but we don't really mean anyone.

About ten years ago I was leading a group of high school seniors through a Bible study sort of like this one. A girl named Christy started coming to church and bringing her boyfriend, Jack. She had been to church a few times as a little girl, but her parents were not married, and the church they were going to made it clear they were no longer welcome. I knew she hadn't been in any kind of group like this before, because the first couple weeks she kept saying things like, "%#@*".* I loved having her there. She was so unassuming when it came to God's grace. Most weeks she was genuinely shocked by what God had to say. After several months of seeing Christy and Jack every week, they stopped coming. I called her and could immediately tell she was not herself. She and Jack showed up at my house later that day, very nervous and unsure of themselves. Jack waited in the other room while she asked me if we could talk. She had trouble getting any words out. Then she finally said, "I want to believe that God can fix anything, but I'm not sure he will want to." We slid down the wall by my front door, and with a quivering lip and bloodshot eyes she continued, "I knew I couldn't come back to church. No one who's good has ever treated me

---

* Okay, maybe not that exactly, but you get the idea.

the same once they knew this about me. I know I've disappointed you. I'm pregnant again. Please tell Jesus how sorry I am, and that I really want him to be with me now more than ever. I know I shouldn't be here with all of you, but I wish I could be. This is my favorite place." She was stopped at the gate and told she didn't have the right qualifications.

Recently I was sent the following letter from a lady in our church who told about an experience she had on the weekend. Here's what she said:

> It was about five minutes till the service started. A young woman, probably late twenties or early thirties, with her ten-year-old son approached me with a "deer in the headlights" look. She had never been here and was clearly anxious. I took her to the check-in counter for her son's class. On the way she told me that she had gotten divorced six years ago and after that she was no longer welcome at the church she had gone to. She hadn't been to church since then. You could hear the guilt and fear in her voice. She was terribly nervous. I shared with her that I had been divorced, and as a single mom I knew how tough it was. Once her son was in class I asked her if she wanted to sit with me in worship. Upon hearing my invitation she asked, "Am I allowed to go inside there?" She pointed to the sanctuary. "I'm not a member." I told her she was.

> When we got to our seats the service had already started and everyone was standing and singing. After the song the worship leader prayed and the first words out of his mouth were, "God, thank you that no matter where our path has taken us in life, you can redeem and forgive us." With that, her tears started to flow and really didn't stop throughout the entire service. I could just see the fear and guilt melt away. At the end of the service you offered an invitation and asked anyone who wanted to talk more about surrendering his or her life to Christ to come down front and meet you. Then we stood for the closing worship songs. Towards the end of the first song she appeared a bit antsy and I assumed that she was probably ready to go get her son and head to the car. I turned to ask her if she was ready to leave, but before I had a chance she opened her mouth first and said, "Do I need to walk down there and talk to him if I want to make that decision?" I told her that would be a good place to start. She simply said, "I want to do that." I asked her if she wanted me to walk with her and she said, "Yes." So, we walked down front.

I can tell you the rest of the story from there. I greet her down front and could see the tears in her eyes. She leaned in to whisper in my ear, "I don't know if I'm allowed to respond to the invitation. I went through a divorce a number of years ago and my old church wouldn't have me." She was stopped at the gate. The cushion got flipped and someone decided her stain was too big.

Jesus has invited anyone to follow him, but when they come to church they find that there is an asterisk. The not so subtle message is *we have to let you in here because Jesus told us to but we are going be keeping an eye on you.* I can't help but wonder if that's how the other disciples must have felt when Jesus invited Matthew. *What about his qualifications? What about his past history? Jesus, surely you don't really mean anyone?* But when Jesus says *anyone*, it turns out what he really means is anyone.

So here Matthew sits at his tax collector's booth, mulling over this rabbi's offer. There is no doubt that Matthew knew what this invitation involved. He understood that it meant giving up everything. He received an invitation, but there was no way he could respond to it and stay the same. Saying yes to following Jesus would mean saying no to his lucrative business.

Anyone can follow but not without giving up everything.

Jesus says,

"Follow me."

Mathew 9:9 simply says:

... and Matthew got up and followed him.

These days, people don't know Matthew as a failure and embarrassment who sold his soul to the Romans for a job. We know Matthew as a follower of Jesus who wrote the first book of the New Testament.

It's important to understand that the grace of God doesn't simply invite us to follow ... it teaches us to follow. Just because Matthew left his past behind and started following didn't mean he was perfect. Far from it. Even after we decide to follow Jesus, we continue to need his grace for the journey. There are plenty of days where I find myself living as a fan, but each morning I receive the same grace-filled invitation that Jesus spoke to Matthew: "Follow me."

So who is invited to follow Jesus? *Anyone.*

Sexual past? *Anyone.*

Social outcast? *Anyone.*

Juvie Hall resident? *Anyone.*

Broken family? *Anyone.*

Bottom of the class? *Anyone.*

Pothead? *Anyone.*

Addict? *Anyone.*

Hypocrite? *Anyone.*

I wonder if you've had a moment like Morgan—a moment like Matthew. The cushion gets flipped. The stain is exposed. You're guilty. You know what you deserve. You know what you have coming. But the words of Jesus are words full of grace. He says, "Follow me." You think, *"There must be a mistake. Doesn't he know who I am? Doesn't he know what I've done?"* Yeah, he knows about the stains. In fact, he died on the cross so that our stains could be washed clean, whiter than snow actually. And because of his grace, we find ourselves at the same crossroads as Matthew.

The invitation of Jesus to follow him begins, *"If anyone ..."*

It turns out that *Anyone* means *Anyone.*

Anyone means me. *Anyone* means you.

not a fan story

Angela Devries

By the time I was only eight years old, Child Protective Services had been notified of my biological parents eleven times. My parents are not well. They both suffer from an illness called schizophrenia. My mother is like a child. She has no way to care for her own needs or mine. My father is dangerous and paranoid. I remember doing a lot of wandering through the streets of downtown. We never really knew if we would eat. My father forbade my mother and me from showering. He thought if we were nasty and smelly, people would avoid us, and he could control us. So my mom and I were not pleasing to the eye (or the nose). The street people that most folks avoid, well, that was us. I missed countless days of school because of my father's anger. I have a lot of disturbing memories of abuse by my father. I remember having things thrown at me, being thrown across the floor, and seeing my mom held at knife point. I know what it is to be intensely frightened. I didn't believe that normal people lived this way; at least I hoped and prayed they didn't. Finally, after my father kidnapped me and took me to Texas, I was placed in foster care. Today, at nineteen, I am part of a wonderful Christian family who adopted me. I accepted Jesus as my Lord when I was eleven and was baptized, surrendering everything to him. My relationship with him is like any relationship; it takes time and energy. He is everything I am living for, and he deserves my honor. What Satan has intended for my harm has backfired on him. His plan was for my destruction. His plan was for me to fail. God's plan has always been for me to prosper. God's plan for me is healing through his Son, Jesus Christ. I still have struggles. There are days I don't feel worthy and have a hard time accepting the love of God my Father. But he continues to show his grace in my life and show me how he is working out all of my past for his glory and my good. Through Jesus, I have forgiven my biological parents. Someday I pray that they can know the living God, like I do. He can bring peace to their troubled minds, and maybe he will use me. My name is Angela Devries, and I am not a fan.

come after me — a passionate pursuit

I want to take you back to the first time you let someone of the opposite sex know that you had feelings for them. For most of us the first time we experienced that was somewhere between fifth grade and seventh grade.

Early on, when we were in first or second grade, we knew there was a difference between boys and girls. We had seen enough Disney movies to know that boys and girls like each other. But instead of thinking about the opposite sex with affection, we thought: *They're gross.* We kept our distance in fear of catching cooties. You get a little older and you find that you're strangely attracted to these gross creatures. You have some feelings, but you don't know what to do with them. Instead of saying, *They're gross*, we say (if we're a boy, at least), *I must hurt them*, and we express our affection by hitting them and causing bodily harm. Then finally it happens; we go from *They're gross* to *I must hurt them* to *I've gotta get me one of those.*

I was in the fifth grade when the first one of my friends made this transition. His name was Nat and he had it bad for a girl in our class. Nat was a good buddy of mine. He was not only in my class at school, but he also lived down the street from me. For years we would ride bikes after school, go swimming in the summer, and go sledding in the winter. But suddenly things changed when Nat got a girlfriend. The rest of us guys thought he had lost his mind. We did not understand why he would sacrifice playing Nintendo for talking on the phone with this girl. We couldn't believe it when he passed love notes in class.

How could this be happening? All I could do was shake my head in disbelief at the sight of Nat sitting at the lunch table, writing a poem to his new girlfriend. It reached a tipping point when one day at recess instead of playing football, we saw Nat playing the hand-clapping game with his girlfriend. A number of us fifth grade boys attempted what would have amounted to "group intervention." We tried to show him the foolishness of his actions. *"Nat, all you do is talk to her or write to her. You spent your hard-earned lawn mowing money on perfume for her. And what is that I smell on you, Nat? It's Old Spice, isn't it? What has happened to you? You're embarrassing yourself."* Nat tried to make us understand how he felt. But I didn't understand how something like that could happen. But something had definitely happened. And then one day I understood. On the first day of the new school year I was sitting at my desk, minding my own business, when a girl named Cari walked into the class. Suddenly everything that Nat had been doing made perfect sense. Cari wasn't a new student, but something happened over the summer and I said to myself, "I gotta get me one of those!" There are some things that have to be experienced to be understood. Some things don't make sense until they happen to you.

The next part of Jesus' invitation to follow him in Luke 9 will make complete sense to followers, but will seem a bit crazy to the fans. In Luke 9:23 Jesus defines the relationship he wants with us. He makes it clear what it means to be a follower:

> If anyone would come after me, he must deny himself and take up his cross daily and follow me.

The phrase I want to draw your attention to is "Come after." It's a phrase that was commonly used in the context of a romantic relationship. When Jesus says "Come after," he's describing a passionate pursuit of someone you love. So the best way to understand what Jesus is wanting from us as followers is to compare how we pursue him to how we would pursue someone with whom we want to have a romantic relationship. Like Nat, most of us have done some illogical and irrational things in the passionate pursuit of someone we love. It's a pursuit that can easily consume our thoughts, our resources, and our energy. That's what Jesus is looking for from a follower when he says "Come after."

Crazy Love Stories

In our world, the relationship we tend to be the most passionate about pursuing is a romantic relationship. We are surrounded by messages that emphasize romantic love as the ultimate human experience. Pursuing love is the subject of countless books. It has inspired beautiful works of poetry and art. It's the plot line of innumerable movies. It is the theme of most every song. Who can forget Whitney Houston singing "I Will Always Love You," or Celine Dion singing "My Heart Will Go On"? Even if you would like to forget, it's difficult. The Beatles sang "And I Love Her." Stevie Wonder declared "You Are the Sunshine of My Life." And then there's that classic from Meat Loaf, "I'd Do Anything for Love." He sings about just how far he would go to pursue that love. "I would do anything for love. I'd run right into hell and back. I would do anything for love ... But I won't do that ..." I never knew what "that" was ... I won't do what? Share the remote, put down the toilet lid, pluck my eyebrows, change my name — I'm not sure what Meat Loaf wouldn't do. But he would do a lot for love. He was willing to run right into hell and back.

Pursuing a romantic love will make us do some crazy things. When I was dating my soon-to-be wife, she borrowed my car to go visit her family about eighty miles away from where we went to college. She had only been gone for a day, but I missed her and wanted to be with her. I woke up in the middle of the night and couldn't stop thinking about her. I wanted to see her and tell her I loved her. I had to do something. My college roommate was sleeping in the bed across the room. I woke him up and told him my dilemma, but he couldn't do much to help because he didn't have a car. Suddenly, I had what seemed like a brilliant idea. I said to him, "What if we just ride bikes over to her house?"

He was up for it, but this new plan presented us with a similar problem as before: neither of us owned bikes. Then my buddy reminded me of the bike racks on campus. We decided it would be fine to "borrow" the bikes for our journey.

Knowing nothing about bicycles, I grabbed the first one I saw, which happened to be a Walmart special. It turns out this is not the bike of choice for an eighty-mile journey down the flat roads of Kansas against constant headwind. After riding for hours, we decided to park our bikes and take a nap in a ditch on the side of the road. While we were sleeping, a state trooper saw us and pulled over to investigate. He woke me up by placing his boot on my shoulder and jostling me awake. I believe his exact words were, "Are you boys smokin' something? What are you doing riding bikes across Kansas?"

I tried to explain: "I wanted to be with my fiancée." He rolled his eyes, shook his head, got in his car, and drove away. He thought I was crazy for doing such a thing. If Nat could see me now.

When we finally made it to Kansas, my wife's response was fairly similar to the state trooper's. She thought I was nuts. But the moment I saw her I knew it was worth it. I could probably tell you a half dozen other stories of how I pursued my wife. I could tell you how I delivered furniture in the heat of the summer for minimum wage, but enjoyed it because the money was going to a wedding ring. I could tell you of the time in college I pulled an all-nighter to finish the research for a thirty-page research paper that she needed to turn in. I could tell you how I donated plasma so I could buy her a dozen roses. There are plenty of examples I could give of how I would come after my wife. It's easy to get mushy and nostalgic looking back at the course of our relationship. I've spent so much energy chasing after her, so much time winning her heart, and I wouldn't trade it for anything. But you know, looking back at my relationship with Christ, I don't have as many stories about chasing after Jesus. The ones I could tell you hardly seem impressive enough to write down here.

Followers should have some *come after* Jesus stories that make people say, *That's crazy.* Many fans didn't grow up thinking about their relationship with Jesus in these terms. Following him was more of a casual weekend thing. You didn't get too carried away with it. You might throw a few bucks in the offering and volunteer to hand out bulletins, but that was about the extent of it. And honestly, that is as far as you wanted it to go. But that's not how Jesus has defined the relationship.

Jesus wants us to understand that following him is a pursuit that requires everything we have. Jesus tells a parable in Matthew 13 called "The Pearl of Great Price." It gives us a picture of what Jesus had in mind when he invited us to *come after* him.

> The kingdom of heaven is like treasure hidden in a field. When a man found it, he hid it again, and then in his joy went and sold all he had and bought that field (Matt. 13:44).

In Bible times people would often bury their savings in the ground. It was considered a safe place, especially during times of war or government upheaval. It would not have been uncommon for someone to bury their treasure in the ground and then be killed while away at war. Jesus describes a scenario where years later a hired hand discovers a buried treasure chest while plowing. He stops, digs it up, brushes it off, and opens the lid. He can't believe his eyes! There are thousands of dollars worth of precious gems glistening in the sun. His heart pounds with excitement. He quickly reburies the treasure and continues working, but the whole time he is carefully plotting his course of action. He is desperate to buy that field so the treasure will be his. That evening he liquidates his assets. He sells everything — his house, his oxen, his cart. Friends and family begin to talk. They think he's lost his mind. It just doesn't make sense. But the truth is, this is the best investment that he could possibly make.

When we discover the life that we can have in Jesus we are to come after him like this man pursued this pearl of great price. Fans will be careful not to get carried away. Followers understand that following Jesus is a pursuit that may cost them everything, but it is the best investment they could ever make. Followers will do some crazy things for love, but fans want to play it safe.

Cohabitating with Jesus

There is a fear among fans that by going all-in, they're going to miss out.

Fans want to have just enough of the pleasure without having to risk feeling any pain. We want to enjoy what's available to us without having to sacrifice for it.

Instead of *come after* we *hold back*. It's not that we don't want a relationship with Jesus; we do. We just don't want it to cost us very much. To go back to the romance metaphor, it's like a man and a woman who have been dating. Things get pretty serious, and she wants to get married. He loves her and doesn't want to lose her, but he doesn't want to get married. He's afraid that if he makes that kind of commitment it will require too much of him or somehow he'll miss out on something better. So he makes the suggestion, "Hey, why don't we move in together?" Translated: "How about I get all the benefits of marriage without having to make any of the commitments and sacrifices?"

That's the approach fans take. Fans say to Jesus, "Hey, why don't we move in together?"

In the satirical magazine called *The Door*, Daniel Murphy suggests that unmarried couples living together should share the following vows:

> I, John, take you, Mary, to be my cohabitant, to have sex with and to share bills with. I'll be around while things are good but I probably won't be if things get tough. If you should get a cold, I'll run to the drugstore for some medicine. If you get sick to the point where you can no longer meet my needs, then I'll have to move on. Forsaking many others I will be more or less faithful to you for as long as it feels good to me. If we should break up, it doesn't mean this wasn't special for me. I commit to live with you for as long as this works out.[2]

Fans are often guilty of offering these kinds of vows to Jesus. *I'll follow you, as long as things are good and you hold up your end of the deal. I'll follow you as long as you don't ask too much of me.* We are afraid to passionately pursue him with our whole hearts because we know that if we make a commitment like that we are putting ourselves on the line. It will require our energy, time, and money.

In the parable of "The Pearl of Great Price" the man sold everything he had to get the treasure, but once he had the treasure did you notice his response?

Then in his joy went and sold all he had and bought that field.

Sacrificing everything he had for the treasure brought him great joy because he knew it was worth it.

Do You Like Me?
☐Yes ☐No ☐Maybe

Remember, these words of Jesus are words of an invitation, not a command. Jesus begins the invitation to *come after* him with the word "if." That indicates that there is a choice in the matter. One of the most basic truths about love is that it can't be forced. If you try and force someone to love you it's almost a guarantee that they won't. One of the reasons some fans don't *come after* Jesus is that they've never been given the opportunity to make their own choice about him. They grew up with a great deal of pressure to be a follower.

These fans never had a chance to pursue because they were always being pushed.

Maybe that's what happened to you.

Your parents decided to have you baptized as a baby, but you've never personally come after him. Or it has been your family's tradition to come to church and call themselves Christians, but you don't ever remember going to church because you wanted to. Mom made you. Dad said you had to. Even as a young adult you still feel pushed. You come to church because your family likes it when you come. The truth is you call yourself a Christian mostly because you always have. Besides, what would people say if you didn't? You're not pursuing a relationship with Jesus; you're just putting up with him to keep up other relationships.

Pursuing Jesus is your choice and Jesus wants to make it clear what you're agreeing to if you respond to his invitation. He will settle for nothing less than to be the great love and pursuit of your life. That's what he wants. At church, we sometimes talk about how "God wants your time," or "God wants your money," or "God wants your worship." But do you understand why we talk about those things?

It's not because God needs your time. He has always been and always will be. It's not because he needs your money. He owns the cattle on a thousand hills. If God needed your money he could take it. It's not that God needs your worship. If you don't worship, the Bible says that the rocks and trees will cry out. The reason we talk about those things is not because God needs or wants those things; it's because he wants you. He wants your love. He longs for you to passionately pursue him, and all those things are *come after* indicators. They are outer signs that point to an inner reality that you love Jesus more than anything else.

Several years ago I heard the testimony of an elderly missionary who was returning from the foreign field to the United States to live out the days he had left with his married daughter in the Midwest. Upon arriving on the California coast he boarded a bus to begin his trip across the country. The first night the bus stopped in Las Vegas. He had been out of the United States for more than thirty years. He had never been to Las Vegas. He checked into a hotel and took a walk down the strip. Although it was close to midnight, it looked like midday, because of all the lights. As he walked down the strip he heard the loud music, saw the amazing hotels, and even went to a car show where he saw the world's finest automobiles. He saw the games being played in the casinos and heard the money coming out of the slot machines. He saw the marquees announcing the amazing entertainers. He saw the drink specials announced and the amazing food advertised in the restaurants. Eventually he went back to his room in the high-rise hotel where he was staying. He entered the room but didn't turn on the light. He walked across the room and opened the curtains. In the quietness of his room he got on his knees in front of the window, looked down at the Vegas strip, then into the more impressive lights of the heavens, and prayed this prayer: "God, I thank you that tonight I haven't seen anything I want more than I want you."

One of the greatest motivations of our love and passionate pursuit of Jesus is a better understanding of how great his love is for us. Being loved causes us to love. We read in 1 John 4:19:

> We love him, because he first loved us (KJV).

The craziest *come after* story of all is when God put on flesh, came to this earth, and died in our place. He took the initiative and pursued you. When we realize the extravagance of his love it begins to change our hearts. We love him, because he first loved us.

Lost That Lovin' Feeling

So what do you do if you're a fan who wants to be a follower but your heart just isn't in it? You want to *come after* Christ with a passionate pursuit, but the truth is you feel apathetic and indifferent. You don't want to feel that way, but you do. I was recently doing some research on what are known as "The Seven Deadly Sins." They don't appear as a list anywhere in Scripture, and I was curious to know how that list was developed. It turns out that years ago the literacy rate was quite low and people weren't reading the Bible for themselves. Some of the early church leaders got together and made a list of the worst sins so at least people would know what not to do. As I was reading about their thinking behind the seven deadly sins I discovered something about the one sin on that list that always seemed out of place to me. They have "sloth" listed as a deadly sin. It has never seemed that deadly to me. I've always thought of sloth as laziness. You know, not changing the channel on the TV because you lost the remote and walking over to the actual TV would be too taxing. I understand that laziness isn't good, but it hardly seems deadly. But I discovered that the word sloth is translated from the word *acedia*. "Sloth" probably isn't the best translation of that word. A better way to convey what the early church leaders were getting at would be to translate the word as "spiritual apathy." You reach a point where you simply say, "I don't care." God loves you and sent his son to die on the cross to forgive your sins and you shrug your shoulders. That's acedia, and it's an epidemic among fans.

The passion is gone. There is no pursuit. Maybe there was a time when you followed Jesus that way, but at some point you lost interest. That's what happened to the Christians in Ephesus. In Revelation 2:4–5 Jesus says this to the church:

> I hold this against you: You have forsaken your first love. Remember the height from which you have fallen! Repent and do the things you did at first. If you do not repent, I will come to you and remove your lampstand from its place.

The NIV says the church had "forsaken" its first love. Other translations say "lost" or "left" their first love. That love refers to a loss of enthusiasm or passion for God himself. In Jeremiah 2:2, God says to his people that he remembers "the devotion of your youth, how as a bride you loved me." Your honeymoon with God should never be over.

So what do you do if you find yourself in a place of acedia, where you want to passionately pursue Jesus but your heart's not in it? Notice what Jesus tells the church in Ephesus. He says to repent and do the things you did at first.

That's a great place to start in your relationship with Christ. Confess the sin of acedia in your life and then start doing the things you did at first. Get on your knees next to your bed and talk to God about your day. Turn on some worship music in your car and sing along. Grab a one-year Bible and start reading and meditating on God's Word. Even if you don't initially feel like doing some of those things it will begin to stir the fire that has grown dim. I would also challenge you to wake up this Sunday morning and gather together with followers who are passionately pursuing Jesus. I think you'll find their passion to be contagious. Recommit your love to God and then passionately pursue him. David put it this way in Psalm 63:8:

> My soul followeth hard after thee ... (KJV).

It's not just here in Luke 9 that Jesus uses the analogy of a romantic relationship to describe the passionate pursuit he wants from his followers. It's not just here in Luke 9 that Scripture uses this as a picture of the relationship God wants with us. It's a common metaphor in both the Old Testament and the New Testament. Why does God use the love between a husband and a wife? I suppose it's because it's the deepest kind of love we can comprehend. But really, the kind of relationship he wants with us is much deeper and richer than that.

When I was back in my hometown visiting my family, I went with my grandma to visit the gravesite where my grandpa was buried. Next to his grave marker was a place reserved for my grandmother. It already has her name on it and the day of her birth. The date of her death will one day be added. If she were honest she would say she is ready for that day right now. She hasn't been the same since my grandpa died. They were married almost sixty years. She misses him so much. We stood in front of his gravesite and she talked about feeling lonely. She told me of how she still reaches over for him at night. Sometimes she finds herself calling to him in the other room, just out of habit. We stood in silence for a few moments and then she said this: "I'm ready. I'm ready to go home and be with ..." and I knew what she was going to say next. She was going to say "... your grandpa." Of course she was going to say that. He was the love of her life. She loved him more than she loved anything. But she didn't say, "I'm ready to go home and be with your grandpa." What she said was, "I'm ready to go home and be with Jesus."

That's the heart of a follower.

not a fan story

Nina Flanagan

My name is Nina Flanagan and my story of passionately pursuing Christ really began because he passionately pursued me.

I grew up in a Christian family with two older brothers and one younger sister. My parents took us to church every Sunday, where I learned all the classic Bible stories and the rules of being a Christian. As I grew up I started singing in the worship band and working with the kids' programs. My family was well known in our church as we were seemingly picture perfect.

The year I graduated from high school my whole world fell apart. Three weeks before prom my mom found out my dad was having an affair, and my dad announced that after my graduation party he was going to leave us.

October 25, 2007, my dad left us. Four days after my eighteenth birthday. I can't even begin to tell you how that felt. Or how it felt the second and third time he left us. At eighteen years old I ended up caring for my sixteen-year-old sister and suicidal mom. Not to mention I was working full time and going to school full time. I couldn't bear going to church; I hated the looks we got. It was hard for me to sit there and praise God when my whole world was falling apart around me. I was so angry. Instead of looking to God for help I tried to fix everything myself.

My mom blamed me for a lot of what happened. I heard a lot of "Nina, if you tell him to come home he will," and "Nina, how come you don't tell him you want him to stay?" The truth was I didn't want him to stay. I thought, *If he doesn't want to be here then I don't want him here.* Eventually my mom would move on and she would go through a slew of guys she met online.

All complete scumbags. My dad was sitting pretty with his girlfriend and her daughters.

I was so angry, and I was sick of people telling me to trust God and that God had a plan for me and *blah, blah, blah*. In fact I was sick of God altogether. I spend my entire teen years following his rules and this is what I had to show for it? My dad had a new family, my mom had creepy boyfriend after boyfriend, and I had nothing. I was just so broken.

I remember one of my aunts came to visit me one day and was once again telling me how much God loved me, and I just looked at her and I said, "I know God's real, and I hear people say he loves me, but I don't feel it anymore. I can't do it anymore. I can't be a Christian. I'm done with God. If he wants me so bad, he can come and get me, but I'm done."

That was November, 2010, and in February, 2011, God came after me.

I was tired of being angry and unhappy. I was frustrated with my life and where I had ended up. God started to call out to me, drawing me back to him. My heart started to soften. One night I laid awake and I just started talking to God. I poured out my heart to him, wanting answers as to why all these things had happened. And I remember God giving me this one word answer: "Job." As I laid there I remembered the story of Job in the Bible. He lost everything but refused to turn away from God. I had realized that instead of pursuing a relationship with him, I had been running from him. I felt so humbled. From that point on I promised God that I would trust him to be in charge and I would follow wherever he leads me. It isn't always easy and I still stumble sometimes with trusting him, but my soul is so at peace, and my heart so full of his love that I can't imagine any kind of life without him. My name is Nina Flanagan and I am not a fan.

deny —
a total surrender

I was at the gym last summer on one of the elliptical machines that faces the window. I was looking out at the parking lot and watching the people come in for a workout before heading home for the day. After a few minutes a guy pulls up and gets out of his car. He's a large guy and it takes some effort for him to get out of his small sedan. He's still in his office clothes, but I watch as he reaches in to grab his gym bag. He puts it over his shoulder and then leans into the car one more time to get something else. He emerges with a cup that has a red spoon in it. You get what's happening? This man is finishing off his Blizzard from Dairy Queen as he walks into the gym for his workout. He stands right outside the window in front of me to take his final bites. I'm pretty sure it was cookie dough. He throws the empty cup in the trash and walks in for his workout. He wanted to get in shape, but he didn't want to make any personal sacrifices.

That's how a fan will try and follow Jesus. A fan will try and accept the invitation of Christ to follow, but they don't want to say no to themselves. In Luke 9:23 Jesus makes it clear that if we are going to follow him, a casual no-strings-attached arrangement isn't a possibility:

> If anyone would come after me, he must deny himself . . .

You can't "come after" Jesus without denying yourself. The phrase "deny himself" isn't just the idea of saying no to yourself—or even resisting yourself. The idea here is that you do not even acknowledge or recognize your own existence.

We talk a lot about the truth that being a Christian means believing in Jesus—but we don't say much about denying ourselves. That is such an unappealing message. How do you deny yourself in a culture that says it's all about yourself?

In Matthew chapter 19 we meet a man whose name we don't know. We learn enough about him from the Gospels that he is referred to as the "Rich Young Ruler." He's followed a path that has led to wealth and power. That's the path that most of us are trying to find. He comes to Jesus with a question. In verse 16 he asks:

> Teacher, what good thing must I do to get eternal life?

You have to give him credit for asking the right question. He wants to know, *how do I get to heaven?* But even the way he asks it reveals the heart of a fan. He says, what must "*I do.*" That word could be translated *acquire* or *earn.* He thinks it's going to be an impressive résumé that will get him in. Eventually Jesus tells this man what he needs to do. In verse 21 Jesus says:

> Sell your possessions and give to the poor, and you will have treasure in heaven. Then come, follow me.

Jesus invites the man to become his follower, but first the man is told to sell all his possessions and give to the poor. He's faced with the choice of following Jesus or keeping his stuff, but he couldn't do both. There was no way to follow Jesus without denying himself.

Many people want to make this story about money, but it's not as much about money as it is about following Jesus. Jesus puts this man at a crossroads. He can follow the path that leads to money, or he can follow Jesus; but he can't follow both.

So what does all this mean for you and me? Is selling everything a requirement to follow Jesus? Well, it may be. In fact, I would say, the more defensive you are of Jesus' words to this man, the more likely it is that Jesus might be saying them to you. What is true is that everyone who follows Jesus will find himself or herself at a similar crossroads as this man in Matthew 19. You won't be able to take the path of following Jesus without walking away from a different path. He wanted to follow Jesus, but when forced to choose between Jesus and his stuff, he chose his stuff. He wouldn't deny himself. What choice will you make?

Living in Denial

A few years ago I was pretty deep into some tribal areas of Africa. One night I finished preaching a message to a crowd of a few dozen people. I presented the gospel and the invitation of Jesus to follow him. There were two young men, probably in their twenties, who accepted Christ and committed to follow him. The following afternoon these two men showed up at the house where we were staying. They each carried a good-sized bag over their shoulder. I went over and asked the local missionary we were staying with why they were here. He explained that these two men would no longer be welcomed by their families or in their village. When I heard that, I was afraid that maybe this was going to be more than they would be willing to go along with. About that time the missionary said to me, "They knew this would happen when they made the decision."

They were choosing Jesus over their families. They were choosing Jesus over their own comfort and convenience, and fans don't do that.

Followers are willing to deny themselves and say, "I choose Jesus. I choose Jesus over my family. I choose Jesus over money. I choose Jesus over my guidance counselor's career advice. I am his completely. I choose Jesus over my game system. I choose Jesus over shopping. I choose Jesus over the person I'm dating. I choose Jesus over looking at porn. I choose Jesus over a new wardrobe. I choose Jesus over my freedom. I choose Jesus over what other people may think of me." A follower makes a decision every day to deny himself and choose Jesus ... even if it costs everything.

When we sacrificially deny ourselves for Christ's sake it is the clearest evidence of our committed love. A committed love is best demonstrated through sacrifice. When we deny ourselves for another person it communicates true love. A friend of mine told of the time he knew that his wife really loved him. He says he was coming into the kitchen for dinner. As he was walking down the hall into the kitchen he could see the table where the food was. His wife didn't know he was watching as she was pouring Pepsi into two glasses, one for him and one for her. There was a little bit of Pepsi left in one two-liter bottle that had been open for more than a week. She also had out a brand-new bottle of Pepsi to open. She filled one glass with the no fizz, flat, old Pepsi, and the second glass with the fresh, newly opened Pepsi. After she had finished pouring he went in and sat down at the table. He wondered to himself, "At whose place is she going to put that flat, stale Pepsi, mine or hers?" When his wife walked over to the table with the two drinks and put the flat Pepsi at her plate, my buddy said he had never felt so loved.

No Exception Clause

One way fans try to follow Jesus without denying themselves is by compartmentalizing the areas of their lives they don't want him to have access to. They try and negotiate the terms of the deal. *I'll follow Jesus, but I'm not going to sell my possessions. Don't ask me to forgive the people who hurt me; they don't deserve that. Don't ask me to save sex for marriage; I can't help my desires. Don't ask me to give a percentage of my money; I worked hard for that cash.* And instead of following Jesus with their money, they follow their own desires. In their relationships, instead of Jesus they follow the latest reality TV show.

They follow Jesus, just not with every area of their lives. In the book *UnChristian*, Barna research reported that 65 percent of eighteen- to forty-two-year-olds in America have "made a personal commitment to Jesus that is still important." On the surface that seems really encouraging. But how many of those are followers? Because their research also showed that only 23 percent of those people believed that sex outside of marriage is wrong. Only 13 percent said getting drunk is a sin. And the list goes on. In other words, 65 percent say they are committed to Jesus, but most of them aren't committed to Jesus in every area of their life. And Jesus never left open the option of selective commitment. There are no exception clauses. You don't get to say, "I follow Jesus — but when it comes to this area of my life, I do things my way." If you call yourself a Christian, by definition you are committing to following Christ with every area of your life. It doesn't mean you will follow perfectly, but you can't say, "I'm a Christian" and then refuse to follow Christ when it comes to certain people or places or practices.

I had just finished preaching one weekend and I walked back to a room where some of our decision guides were talking to people who had made a spiritual decision. I noticed a woman who seemed pretty angry and upset with the person talking to her about her decision. Her husband or boyfriend was trying to calm her down. I went over to see what the problem was. She and her boyfriend had come forward to become members of the church, but they were living together. They were told what the Bible taught about honoring the marriage bed and reserving sex for marriage. They were asked if they would be willing to repent of their sin and not live together until they were married, but they were not happy about this choice they were being asked to make. I sat down and explained that you don't have to have your life together to become a Christian or be a part of the church, but you must be willing to repent of your sins. She explained that they weren't going to do that. The problem was they wanted to be called Christians without actually making an effort to follow Christ.

I saw a report on MSNBC about a group of new vegetarians. They interviewed one of the new vegetarians, a young woman named Christy Pugh. One of her quotes captures the viewpoint of this group. She said, "I usually eat vegetarian. But I really like sausage." She represents a growing number of people who eat vegetarian but make some exceptions. They don't eat meat, unless they really like it. As you can imagine, the real vegetarians aren't real happy about the new vegetarians. They put pressure on the new vegetarians to change their name. And so here's the name they chose for themselves: flexetarians. As I watched the report I realized something; I'm a flexetarian. I absolutely refuse to eat meat, unless it's being served. Christy explains it this way: "I really like vegetarian food, but I'm just not 100 percent committed."[3]

"Flexetarian" is a good way to describe how many people approach their commitment to Christ. And that's the way many Christians approach their commitment to Jesus and the Bible. *I really like Jesus —but I don't really like serving the poor—I'm not real big into the idea of going to church—but my resources are spoken for. I love Jesus —but don't ask me to save sex for marriage. I love Jesus—but don't ask me to forgive the person who hurt me. I love Jesus—but I'm not 100 percent committed.* They call themselves Christians. They follow Jesus, but they've made some exceptions. So when bacon is on the menu, their commitments can be adjusted.

Following Jesus requires a complete and total commitment. What the Rich Young Ruler is really committed to is revealed when he refuses to deny himself. He wanted to say yes to following Jesus without saying no to himself. He wanted to be close enough to Jesus to have eternal life, but not so close that it required personal sacrifice.

Reading the Fine Print

For many Christians the concept of denying themselves was not part of the deal. They grew up with the message that such a radical decision really isn't necessary. So they signed up to follow Jesus, but if denying themselves was part of the explanation, it was definitely the fine print. That's especially true of American Christians. In part, this is due to the collision of Christianity with American capitalism. It has created a culture of consumers in our churches. Instead of approaching their faith with a spirit of denial that says, "What can I do for Jesus?" they have a consumer mentality that says, "What can Jesus do for me?"

There is a business book written by Ken Blanchard called *Raving Fans*. The book teaches businesses how to make the customer so happy and feel so important that they become "Raving Fans" of the company. Ken is a committed Christian and a friend of our church. One of our staff leaders suggested that the staff read his book as a way to better serve our members. While it is an excellent business book and there were some good takeaways for the church, as I read it there were a number of times I thought, "This is a great way to recruit customers, but a dangerous way to call followers."

Many churches have become companies that measure success by the number of customers they have attracted. And how do we get more customers? By trying to make the customer feel comfortable, important, and happy. We want the product (in this case following Jesus) to come off as appealing and as comfortable as possible. So when someone comes in "church shopping" we try and show them what we have to offer.

Can you see why this undermines the invitation of Jesus to deny ourselves? The church sends the message, "Whatever you want you can get it here." The invitation of Jesus is, "Give up everything." The message of the church sounds less like "Deny yourself" and more like Burger King's slogan, "Have it your way." I fear the result is often a church full of raving fans, but not many followers.

Contrast the image of consumer with a much different biblical image that Scripture uses to describe followers. The Bible would describe a follower as a "slave." That is the exact opposite of a consumer. The image of slave provides a picture of what "deny yourself" looks like.

A slave has no rights. A slave has no possessions to call their own. A slave in Jesus' day didn't even have a personal identity. A slave doesn't get time off or get to clock out at the end of the day. A slave doesn't get to negotiate. But "slave" is the way many of the followers of Christ introduced themselves.

When Peter began 2 Peter, he didn't introduce himself by saying, "Peter, a best friend of Jesus, present at the Mount of Transfiguration, preacher on the day of Pentecost." Instead he simply says, "Simon Peter, a slave ..." (NLT). John, Timothy, and Jude all give themselves the same title. James doesn't begin his letter by saying, "James, the half brother of the Son of God." He begins by saying, "James, a slave of God and of the Lord Jesus Christ" (NLT). When Paul wrote to the church in Rome he wrote to people who hated the word *slave*. We find it offensive these days because of what happened in the past, but for the readers of Romans, the wounds and the pain of slavery were fresh. And yet Paul's letter to the Romans begins this way: "Paul, a slave of Christ Jesus" (NLT). Really? Why not say, "Paul, educated by Gamalial, spoken to on the road to Damascus, bestselling author of... the Bible?" But all he says is, "Paul, a slave of Jesus Christ."

One of Christ's followers who is a hero to me is Bill Bright. He was the founder of Campus Crusade for Christ. He wrote the tract called *The Four Spiritual Laws* that presents the gospel. More than 2.5 billion copies have been distributed worldwide. He was central to the "Jesus Film," which has been seen by more than 4 billion people in 660 languages around the world. But if you were to visit his gravesite, you would find only three words on his tombstone: Slave for Jesus.

One of the reasons it's so hard for us to deny ourselves is because the whole idea seems to go against our greatest desire in life. Most everyone would say what they want more than anything else is to be happy. We're convinced that the path to happiness means saying yes to ourselves. Indulgence is the path to happiness, so to deny ourselves seems to go in the opposite direction of what will make us happy. The right to pursue happiness seems to be in direct conflict with the call to deny.

Most of us grew up in homes where we were taught to study hard in school and in college so we could get a good job and make lots of money and live in a big house, drive a nice car, and enjoy great vacations. When you were asked as a child what you wanted to be when you grew up, your answers generally reflected that influence.* But no one ever says, "When I grow up, I want to be a slave." But that is what the Bible calls us to. The Bible would teach that the highest calling for you is to be a slave who denies himself and follows Jesus.

Understanding my identity as a slave was huge for me. Ironically it wasn't until I understood that I was a slave that I finally found freedom. I want to explore this a little more with you, but it will mean you hanging with me for a few quick word studies. The word "slave" is a common word used for followers, so it only makes sense that Jesus

---

* My wife asked my three-year-old son, "So what do you want to be when you grow up?" My son answered, "A football player!" But then he threw something else in there he had never mentioned. He said, "When I grow up, I want to be a mermaid." What? I finally said, "That's merman, buddy, merman."

is often called "Lord." When we read in the New Testament that Jesus is called Lord we equate that with his Divinity. We think of "Lord" as a synonym for "God." But in the New Testament when followers refer to Jesus as Lord, that is not a reference to his divine status or his heavenly residence. The word they were using wasn't *Yahweh*. Instead the word that is translated as Lord in the New Testament is most often the word *Kurios*. It shows up hundreds of times. And *Kurios* is a slavery word. *Kurios* is the word given to the master or owner of the slave.

The other word we need to understand is the word *doulos*. That's the word used to describe a follower. The definition of this word isn't difficult. It is a word that is most accurately translated as slave. Really "slave" is the only way the word should be translated. That word appears about one hundred thirty times in the New Testament. For a number of different reasons that word is usually translated as "servant" in Scripture. But the most literal translation is "slave." That's without question the way the readers would have heard it. But there is a huge difference.

A servant works for someone; a slave is owned by someone.

With these words in mind, what I'm about to say seems like it should be pretty obvious but may come as a surprise to fans:

You can't call Jesus Lord without declaring yourself his slave.

Does that make sense? If you hear a little girl in the mall call me "Dad," then she has identified herself as my daughter. When you call Jesus "Lord," you aren't saying, "He's the teacher — and I'm the student." You are saying, "He's the master and I am the slave." That's what it means to deny yourself.

I was reading about a group of missionaries in what is now Surinam in South America. They wanted to reach the inhabitants of a nearby island with the gospel. Most of these islanders were slaves on the large plantations that covered the island. The plantation owners would only allow slaves to talk with other slaves. The missionaries had no way to reach them. So here's what they did; they sold themselves into slavery. Working in bondage in the harsh conditions of a tropical climate, they reached many of them with the gospel. That seems crazy, but here's what you have to understand—they simply became what they already were.

Signing Up for Slavery

When we accept the invitation to deny ourselves and follow Jesus, we become his slaves. That's a completely different way to look at slavery. We think of slavery as something you're forced into, but Jesus invites us to deny ourselves. Why would anyone ever want to be a slave? Actually, it was rare, but in the Old Testament we read of people who chose to be slaves. They were called "Bondslaves." These were people who were set free after being a slave for six years, but they decided they wanted to stay a slave. Deuteronomy 15:16 – 17 explains, "But if your servant says to you, 'I do not want to leave you,' because he loves you and your family and is well off with you, then take an awl and push it through his ear lobe into the door, and he will become your servant for life." A bondslave is how many of the New Testament writers describe themselves. They had willingly become slaves. Luke chapter 1 tells us that when Mary is told that she would be giving birth to the Messiah, her response (recorded in verse 38) is, "I am the Lord's servant." But the word is "bondslave."

Choosing to become a bondslave was an act of complete self-denial. A bondslave gave up all their rights to the master. He is agreeing to give up all his possessions to the master. A slave couldn't pick and choose what was part of the deal. He couldn't say, *"I'm going to be a slave but I want to keep the car, and I need every other weekend off. I need to have a room with a view."* It wasn't a negotiation. A bondslave would say, "Everything I have, everything I am, I sign over to you." That's what Jesus was wanting from the rich young ruler.

But why would anyone ever choose to be a slave? Who signs up for that? Well did you notice in Deuteronomy 15 what the motivation is for someone to choose slavery? Look at it again. "But if your servant says to you, 'I do not want to leave you,' because he loves you and your family and is well off with you . . ." A slave realizes as crazy as it might seem to everyone else, as ridiculous as it might appear to those who don't understand, he's going to choose a life of slavery. He loves his master and realizes that he's better off as a slave.

So out of love we become a slave to Jesus. When you finally surrender all that you have and all that you are you will discover the strangest thing. It's only by becoming a slave to Jesus that we ever truly find freedom.

We think that by denying ourselves we will miss out, but just the opposite is true. In Matthew 19 when Jesus invited the Rich Young Ruler to sell everything and follow him, we read his response in verse 22:

He went away sad, because he had great wealth.

That seems like such a strange statement. He went away sad because he was rich. But he should be sad because he chose to follow the wrong directions. He thought denying himself of all of his stuff would make him sad, but the truth is it's only when we deny ourselves that we truly discover the joy of following Christ.

Jesus invites you to deny yourself. He invites you to be a slave. But as a slave may I tell you about my master. My master will provide for you. He owns the cattle on a thousand hills; he can take care of your needs. My master will protect you. He speaks and even the wind and the waves obey him. My master has the power to forgive sins. If being a slave to sin has left you broken and bruised and you find your life is in pieces, my master can take the pieces of your life and turn them into a beautiful mosaic. If you are worn out and exhausted, my master gives rest to those who are weary and heavy burdened.

One more thing. When you became a slave to my master, he makes you his son. He makes you his daughter. He calls you a friend.

Instead of raving fans, may our churches be filled with slaves who are cleverly disguised as waiters, skaters, artists, singers, athletes, and students.

There is a legal document called a "quitclaim deed" that captures the spiritual decision I'm challenging you to make. A quitclaim deed is used when a person is signing over all rights to property or a possession that they once had a share in. When they sign a quitclaim deed they are giving up whatever claim they once had. They are surrendering all their rights. When Jesus invites us to follow there's not a lot of paperwork involved, but he's looking for some kind of a quitclaim deed. When you decide to follow him you are signing over your house, your car, your cash, your education, your friendships, your future, and anything else that you once laid claim to. You have no more rights and nothing can be withheld. You deny yourself and sign a quitclaim deed on your life.

Millard Fuller tells of becoming a millionaire by the age of twenty-nine. He had, he says, bought his wife everything she could possibly want. But one day he came home to a note that announced that she had left him. Millard went after her. He found her on a Saturday night in a hotel in NYC. They talked into the wee hours of the morning as she poured out her heart and made him see that the "things" that our society says are supposed to be so satisfying had left her cold. Her heart was empty and her spirit was burned out. She was dead inside and she wanted to live again. Kneeling at their bedside in that hotel room, Millard and Linda decided to sell everything they had and dedicate themselves to serving poor people.

The next day being Sunday, they found the nearest Baptist church and went there to worship and thank God for their new beginning. They shared with the minister and told him about what had happened to them and the decision they had made. Ironically, the minister told them that such a radical decision was not really necessary. Millard said, "He told us that it was not necessary to give up everything. He just didn't understand that we weren't giving up money and the things that money could buy. We were giving up, period." Millard and Linda started an organization you're probably familiar with—Habitat for Humanity.

That's what the story of the Rich Young Ruler is really about. It's not just about giving up money and the things that money can buy; it's about giving up, period. That's what it means to deny yourself and follow Christ.

not a fan story

Jordan Piper

My name is Jordan Piper. I am twenty years old, born and raised in North Carolina. I was by no means brought up in a "church family," but my parents believe in God. My grandparents encouraged us to attend our rather small Southern Baptist church. We went sporadically throughout the year and I attended vacation Bible school every summer.

I've played basketball, baseball, and football since the age of five. My dad was always my rec-league coach for all three sports; this had a positive and negative effect on me. Although my dad was a great coach, he criticized me for every wrong move I made. It was very embarrassing to hear my dad screaming at me from across the basketball court or football field. Often, that traveled back home as well. My dad liked to drink alcohol. When he did, he often called me degrading names and made fun of me in any way he could think of. I eventually became extremely self-conscious and insecure.

I can remember many more times of my parents cursing each other out than enjoying each other's presence. My parents ended up getting a divorce at the end of my eighth grade year. I quit all the team sports that I had spent my entire life playing and training for. I lost interest in the things I once loved. My relationship with my father steadily declined, and I put all the blame on myself. I would think, "What could I have done differently so that my parents would still be together?" I became depressed and spent many nights crying myself to sleep.

My mom and I moved to another city, and got a fresh start. I started playing football again and was partying on Friday nights after my football games. I became engaged in sexual relationships with girls. Some were my girlfriend at the time. Some were just "casual" hookups. During this time I was doing the church thing and was a fan of Jesus; but I wasn't even trying to live a sincere, Christian life. As years passed by, I continued down this same path. I became heavily involved with a group of friends I met through the automotive industry that loved money, cars, partying, and sex. I was nineteen years old and had my car featured on the most popular car website in the world. But three hours after the photo shoot this car that I had poured so much time and money into was damaged. I was devastated. It was like God slapped me in the face and woke me up to what I was giving my life to, and I realized the dead-end road I was on.

I plugged in to the college ministry at the church I sometimes attended. I began to make some new friends and went on a mission trip to Haiti. My life was changed forever. I'm ready to follow no matter what that means or where he leads. In fact, in a few months I'm leaving for Haiti again, but this time I'm staying for six months.

I'm Jordan Piper, and I am not a fan.

take up your cross daily — an everyday death

When I was twenty-one years old, my wife and I moved to Los Angeles County, California, to start a new church. I read as much as I could about planting a church, but had no experience and was in way over my head. I filled a notebook with questions about how to go about starting a new church. What seemed clear to me was that if a new church is to be successful then people have to come. The more people that come the more successful the church will be was such an obvious equation, I decided that there was only one question that really needed to be answered:

How do I get as many people as possible to come to this new church?

The answer to this question soon led me into reading some business books that were all about marketing your product and attracting customers. And without making a conscious decision to do so, I set out to start a new church like a person would start a new business.

I learned that in starting a new business it's important to sit down and put together a business plan. Part of a good business plan is to put together a marketing strategy. A good marketing strategy relies upon, among other things, a slogan and a symbol that will attract potential customers. You want them to see your symbol and hear your slogan and think to themselves, "That's what I've been looking for—I want to be a part of that."

The right slogan can not only bring your company to a customer's mind but also create desire for the product. The symbol, or logo, of the company should be memorable and appealing. Let me give you a few examples of slogans and you try and guess the company. You can check your answers below:*

- *Melts in your mouth not in your hand.*
- *It's everywhere you want to be.*
- *The Ultimate Driving Machine.*
- *Just do it.*
- *It keeps going, and going, and going . . .*
- *You're in good hands with . . .*

How did you do? Chances are you know most of those companies and have been, or at least would like to be, associated with them in some way. Not only do you know their names, my guess is you would be able to picture the symbol that represents each of those companies. The symbols represent fulfillment, pleasure, satisfaction, victory, style, and status. Those companies have worked hard to develop a slogan and a symbol that will be appealing and attract as many people as possible.

With that in mind, what would you identify as the slogan and symbol for followers of Christ? Jesus lays it out in Luke 9:23 when he extends an invitation to follow him.

If anyone would come after me, he must deny himself and take up his cross daily and follow me.

The slogan for followers of Christ could accurately be captured this way:

Come and Die.

Well, at least it gets your attention. Not really the kind of slogan that draws people in. It sounds like a horror flick that is released around Halloween. It's not a slogan people flock to; it's a slogan people flee from. Nobody wants to talk about death. We don't even like the word death. When someone dies we say, *"They've passed on/ they've gone ahead/ they're no longer with us/ they've kicked the bucket/ they've*

---

*M&M's / Visa / BMW / Nike / Energizer / Allstate

bought the farm/ they're pushing up daisies/ they're swimmin' with the fish." Death is so final; it's so complete. Exactly. As Bonhoeffer put it, "When Christ calls a man, he bids him come and die."

The symbol for followers of Christ isn't any better. It is a cross. An instrument of torture and death is the image that represents followers of Jesus.

It seems like there were other options that Jesus could have gone with. Why not a dove? It represents peace. What about a shepherd's staff? It's a symbol of protection. Or a rainbow; it represents hope and promise. Why choose two bloody beams nailed together? If you want to attract customers, an image of perhaps the most brutal means of execution ever devised isn't a great place to start.

We've tried to make the most of it. We turned it into ornaments and pieces of jewelry. But to those who were hearing these words of Jesus in Luke 9 the invitation to take up a cross would have been both offensive and repulsive.

For the Jews, the cross was a means of execution that the Romans used to force them into submission. It was a symbol of the Romans' power and strength. Every once in a while a group of Jewish rebels would rise up and lead a revolt against the Roman oppression. The Romans would crucify those involved in the rebellion, sometimes crucifying as many as two thousand at a time along the dusty roads of Palestine.

The cross was **a symbol of humiliation**. In the ancient world, the Romans had a number of ways to carry out an execution. They knew how to execute people very cheaply. Some people would be executed by fire and others would be stoned. Still others would be killed with a stroke of the sword. They might simply give a person a drink of hemlock. Crucifixion on the other hand required four soldiers and a centurion to oversee. It was much more expensive. So why crucifixion? They would use it when they wanted to publicly humiliate the person being crucified. They wanted to make a public statement that this person has no power and is nothing. We read in Scripture how the soldiers humiliated and mocked Jesus. They spit on him. The Bible says he was crucified *naked* on a cross. The Bible says in Philippians 2 that followers are to have the same attitude as Jesus who made himself nothing. Here is Jesus. He is the Creator, the Savior, and the King of kings. And now the one who had everything, made himself nothing. He, who had the world at his feet, chose to come and wash the feet of the world. If we are going to follow him it means humbly taking up a cross and making ourselves nothing.

The cross was a **symbol of suffering**. Before crucifying a criminal, it was common for the Romans to beat them the way they did Jesus. For this scourging, the man was stripped of his clothing, and his hands were tied most often to an upright post. The idea was that a person would have their hands tied around a post so that the flesh on their body would be stretched out tightly in preparation for the scourging. The number of lashes wasn't what the Romans paid attention to; they were experts in beating a person just to the edge of death. After being beaten beyond recognition, the Roman soldiers put the patibulum of the cross, which is the horizontal beam, on the man's back. Perhaps some of the vertebrae were exposed from the flogging. This 125-pound beam was placed on his open wounds. It's no wonder Jesus had a difficult time carrying the cross as he stumbled down the narrow roads of the *Via Dolarosa* (or the Way of Suffering). Taking up your cross and following Jesus can and will bring pain and suffering.

You can't carry a cross without suffering.

You can't carry a cross without suffering.

There is no comfortable way to carry a cross; I don't care how you position it. I often talk to people who are convinced that some suffering or pain in their lives is an indication that they must not be following Jesus. After all, if they are following Jesus, the Son of God, doesn't it follow that things in life are going to unfold smoothly? There is this junk theology floating around out there that points to difficulties as evidence that you must not be following Jesus. The biblical reality is that when people say yes to following Jesus, they are agreeing to carry a cross, and that will be painful at times.

There are a number of Scriptures that do more than hint at the fact that if you are following Jesus it will cost you something.

Luke 6:22: *Blessed are you when men hate you, when they exclude you and insult you and reject your name as evil, because of the Son of Man.*

2 Timothy 3:12: *Everyone who wants to live a godly life in Christ Jesus will be persecuted.*

Philippians 1:29: *For it has been granted to you on behalf of Christ not only to believe on him, but also to suffer for him.*

And here's the question that is keeping me awake these days: *Am I really carrying a cross if there is no suffering and sacrifice?* When is the last time that following Jesus cost you something? When is the last time it cost you a relationship? When is the last time following Jesus cost you a little social status? When is the last time following Jesus cost you getting a part or making a grade? When is the last time you were mocked for your faith? Forget about having our lives threatened ... When is the last time you went without a meal for the sake of the gospel? Can you really say you are carrying your cross if it hasn't cost you anything? Take a second and answer that question in your mind. Has it cost you anything? If there is no sacrifice involved, if you're not at least a little uncomfortable, then there is a good chance that you aren't carrying a cross.

Ultimately the cross was a **symbol of death**. When Jesus gets to Golgotha, the place of the skull, the soldiers take the horizontal beam and attach it to the vertical beam to make a cross. His hands are nailed to the tree. Next the soldiers would have nailed the feet of Jesus to the cross. Hours later a spear was thrust into his side to confirm his death. Jesus invites followers to die to themselves. We die to our own desires, our pursuits, and our plans. When we become followers of Jesus, that is the end of us.

> Am I really carrying a cross if there is no suffering and sacrifice?

A cross, more than anything else, represented death. For those carrying a cross the outcome is certain. "Dead man walking" is a phrase sometimes used to describe a person on death row, and the expression is certainly appropriate for a follower carrying a cross. Jesus takes the most despised and rejected symbol of his time and says, "If you want to follow me, take this up." He invites us to die.

Jesus makes it clear that following him means taking up your cross and dying to yourself. That's what a follower is committing to. I can only imagine the awkward tension as Jesus lays out this expectation for his followers. Unfortunately, many churches today have decided that this message is too uncomfortable and the cross is too offensive. As a result, there are many fans who call themselves followers, but they're not carrying a cross.

When I was out of town speaking at a church on the West Coast, I had a man come to me expressing concern because his daughter was getting ready to be married to a young man who was an atheist. The father pleaded with me to meet with his soon-to-be son-in-law. I got the young man's cell number and called him on my way back to the hotel. I told him who I was and asked if we could grab lunch before my plane left the next day. To my surprise he agreed. A pastor having lunch with an atheist sounds like the beginning of a joke, but he and I hit it off immediately. We talked for several hours, and after he told me his story, I presented the gospel to him. It was the first time he had heard most of what I said. At the end of the lunch we prayed together and he repented of his sins and confessed that he believed that Jesus was the Son of God. I gave him my cell phone number and connected him to the local pastor. I was amazed that God crossed our paths at just the right time. About six weeks later I was thrilled to talk to the pastor of the church and hear that this young man's faith and commitment to Christ had grown rapidly. I didn't hear any more about him for more than a year. Then one day my phone rang and he was on the other line. He told me that he had been married for eight months and things were going well. But he went on to explain that his father-in-law was upset with him and he wanted to ask me what he should do. His father-in-law felt like he needed to "throttle-back" his faith. Apparently, he had been taking seriously God's Word in the area of tithing and his father-in-law felt like that money would be better used saving up for a house. He had also expressed disapproval of this young man's decision to not work on Sunday so he could worship God in the church. And his father-in-law told him, "I'm really glad you've become a Christian, but Jesus never wanted you to become a fanatic."

In other words, *I'm glad you're following Jesus, but why don't you put the cross down.* Jesus makes it clear that the road you take when you follow him is called *The Via Dolarosa.*

History and church tradition tell us that many of those who followed Jesus when he was here on earth ended up on that road. According to tradition, Matthew was killed by a sword in Ethiopia. Mark died in Alexandria, Egypt, after being dragged by horses through the streets until he was dead. Luke was hanged in Greece. Peter was crucified upside down. Thomas was stabbed with a spear in India during a missionary trip. Jude, the brother of Jesus, was killed with arrows when he refused to deny his faith in Christ. James was beheaded in Jerusalem.

A decision to follow Jesus is a decision to die to yourself.

Snuggie Theology

Contrast the symbol of the cross with our love for comfort. Most of us commit our time and our resources to make our lives as comfortable as possible. We are by nature comfort seekers, not cross bearers. We are the people of the Lazyboy, the country club, the day spa, and the Snuggie. Have you seen the Snuggie advertised? It's a blanket with sleeves. At first I thought it was a ridiculous idea. But the more I saw the Snuggie the more I wanted one. When my wife asked me what I wanted for Valentine's Day, I was surprised by the words that came out of my mouth. I said, "I want a Snuggie." That's a phrase you never plan on saying as a grown man. I was excited about a blanket with sleeves. When it finally arrived, I put it on and thought, "Wait a second, I already have one of these. This is just a bathrobe that you put on backwards." Contrast the image of the Snuggie with the image of the cross. One represents ease and comfort; the other represents pain and sacrifice. It's no surprise that more than twenty million Snuggies have been sold. Unfortunately, many churches have developed Snuggie Theology, where they try and make sure everyone is as comfortable as possible. The Snuggie Theology promises health and wealth to all who follow Jesus. Instead of promising you a cross to carry, they promise you a luxury car and a beautiful home. The message may still be preached from the Bible in a church, but certain parts are left out, and if you look around my guess is that you won't see any crosses in the building.

You start to see the consequences of the Snuggie Theology when someone gets dumped, or they don't get accepted to the school, or their family falls apart. They start to question God because according to the gospel that was presented to them, God isn't holding up his end of the deal. One of the elders at our church described in a sentence how this happens. He said, *"What you win them with is what you win them to."* When we win them with a Snuggie Theology, they are not going to be happy when they are told to take up a cross.

Let me give you an example of how this works. I read a for sale ad from someone who wanted to sell a car. It went something like this:

> This car runs okay and the tires are pretty new, but that's about it. It has no radio, the acceleration is sluggish, the clutch is sticky, the back-hood door latch doesn't work (you must prop it up with a stick), and its gas mileage is probably no better than about 10–15 miles per gallon. In general, it's an American car, made during the time when American cars were built VERY poorly. The $500 price quoted above is just because all my friends tell me that a running car MUST be worth at least $500. I suppose I'll bargain with you to lower the price.

But there could be a much more appealing ad for the same car:

> With nearly new tires this car really holds the road. An empty space is available, allowing you to put in the stereo system of your choice. With acceleration like this, you won't have to worry about getting pulled over. A special stick is included at no additional cost that conveniently props up the back hood. When you buy this American-made car you're supporting our country and the freedom we enjoy. Will sacrifice for $499.99.

This is how many sermons are presented. I think a lot of well-intended preachers adopt a Snuggie Theology when they find themselves in churches of a few hundred people and discover an incredible pressure to grow. The attendance isn't what was hoped for, and the offerings are down. Before they know it has happened they gauge success not by their faithfulness to God's Word but by the weekend stats. And so the sermons get sanitized. Scripture gets edited. The cross gets covered up. The sermons are often about salvation, but never about surrender. Often about forgiveness, but never about repentance. Often about living, but never about dying.

I am sorry to say that I know this from personal experience. As a preacher you all too easily find yourself presenting the parts of the Bible that will be more popular. The parts that you don't think will be as well received are dressed up with creative language in an attempt to try and distract from the offensiveness. Instead of the uncompromised and unfiltered truths from God's Word, people are given a neutered and more easily accepted version. In doing so we rob the gospel of its power and the people of the life God has for them.

I remember reading the story of a man named Robert Courtney. He was convicted of diluting the medication of cancer patients in order to make a profit. Over a period of about nine years he diluted an estimated 98,000 prescriptions of medications affecting some 4,200 patients. At least seventeen cancer patients died after receiving diluted formulation of chemotherapy. He made some nineteen million dollars from the fraud. Robert was sentenced to thirty years in prison. A man had been entrusted with the responsibility of handing out lifesaving medication; but for the sake of personal gain, diluted it to the point where it couldn't help people.

That's a picture of what many preachers, myself included, are sometimes guilty of doing. Perhaps not with selfish motives, but the outcome is the same. In fact the stakes are much higher.

Jesus didn't come to this earth so that you would be better behaved or to tweak your personality or to fine-tune your manners or smooth out your rough spots. Jesus didn't even come to this earth to change you. The truth of the gospel is that Jesus came so that you could die.

In *Mere Christianity*, C. S. Lewis puts it this way:

> Christ says, "Give me all. I don't want so much of your time and so
> much of your money and so much of your work: I want you. I have not
> come to torment your natural self, but to kill it. No half-measures are
> any good. I don't want to cut off a branch here and a branch there.
> I want to have the whole tree down. I don't want to drill the tooth, or
> crown it, or stop it, but to have it out."

The slogan is "Die Daily," and the symbol is the cross. That's a
message that a friend of mine missed. He was recently telling me
about how he became a Christian. Someone came up to him and said,
"If you died tonight, do you know where you would go?" My friend
was a little unnerved by the question and talked to the person, and
by the end of the night my friend accepted Jesus as his Savior. I was
enjoying hearing the story but my friend said to me, "The problem is I
didn't die that night." I didn't quite understand what he meant by that.
He explained that there was another question he wished the guy had
asked him. My friend explained to me that when he accepted Christ
he knew that when he died he would receive eternal life, but no one
told him that when he accepted Christ he was making a decision to
die right then. He got the message that when he died he would go to
heaven to be with God, but it was ten years later before he understood
that death starts now.

I've been around my share of dead people. I've been in the room
before the coroner comes in. I have sat with a family as their father
and husband took his last breath. I have stood next to many open
caskets as friends and family walked by to say good-bye. And I don't
mean to be uncouth, but I've noticed something about dead people.
People who are dead don't seem to care very much what other people
think of them. Dead people aren't concerned with how nice their
clothes are. Dead people aren't caught up in how much money is in
their account. Dead people aren't at all thinking about getting the Ivy
League scholarship. The point is that death is the ultimate surrender
of yourself and all that you have. When you're dead, you're no longer
concerned with your life.

Choosing Death

When Jesus calls us to follow him, he says, *"Take up your cross ..."*
The word "take" indicates that dying is a choice we make. That's not
typically how we think of death. We think of death as something that
we don't choose; it happens against our will. Scientists talk about
what's called the "Survival Instinct" within each of us. When our lives
are threatened, self-preservation can drive us to extreme measures.
That's why this slogan of *Come and Die* and this symbol of a cross
aren't just counter-cultural, they're counter-intuitive. Nothing about it
makes sense or feels right. It goes against our Survival Instinct.

When I was a boy in grade school, at recess we would play a game
many of you are familiar with called "King of the Hill." We had a small
hill behind the school and the boys would push and shove each other
down, and the person standing on top of the hill when the whistle blew
at the end of recess was the king. Forgive me for being a bit proud of
my fourth grade accomplishments, but I was the undisputed king of
King of the Hill. I had a significant advantage in that I got my growth
early and was the same size then as I am now. But I loved being the
king. I was on top while everyone else was in the dirt.

I remember one day we got a new student in class. This student was
bigger than me and taller than me, and ... she was a girl. At first I
wasn't scared, because I thought, "What girl would ever want to play
King of the Hill?" But you would have to have seen Barbara. She was
wearing cowboy boots. And the first day of recess, I saw her spit,
which was not a good sign. I started to worry about my reign as King
of the Hill when Barbara ate glue in art class. And sure enough at
recess that day she wanted to play King of the Hill. In hindsight we
clearly should have established a "no girls allowed" rule, but it was
too late. And Barbara dug her boots into the ground, spit, and came
after me. And when the whistle blew that day, there was a new king ...
or ... um ... queen of the hill. I had been dethroned by a girl. It was a
horrible feeling. I went to the school secretary and told her I didn't feel
good. My mom came and picked me up and I went home for the day.

We never choose to make ourselves less. We fight and claw our way to the top. Should we find ourselves down it's only because we were forced into that position. We never willingly relinquish our title as king. But when the King of kings died on a hill called Calvary it was an example for us to follow.

The phrase "cross to bear" is probably one that you've heard used before. "Cross to bear" is an expression that is used when a challenging situation or responsibility has been put on us against our will. The phrase "cross to bear" gets used for everything from dealing with a learning disability to really slow internet speed. But the idea is that through no choice of your own you have to deal with an especially difficult and challenging situation. But for a follower of Christ a cross is not forced upon us, it is taken up. We don't bear a cross—we willingly pick it up and carry it. Jesus sets this example. In John 10:18 Jesus says, *"No one takes it from me, but I lay it down of my own accord."*

Dying Daily

Jesus invites you to *"take up your cross ..."* That is often where we leave his invitation. But the next word makes all the difference. The word is "daily." *"... take up your cross daily ..."* Every day we make a decision that we will die to ourselves and live for Christ. Dying to ourselves is not a one-time decision. It's a daily decision. That's the most challenging part of dying.

Think of your life as a one hundred dollar bill. Most of us think of dying to ourselves as this one big moment where we hand over our one hundred dollar bill. I don't want to take away from that moment. That moment of salvation is the most important moment of your life. But to see following Jesus as a one-time decision is like saying after your wedding, "Now that I'm married, it's back to life as usual." There is more to being a husband or wife than a wedding ceremony. Instead of thinking of our lives as a one hundred dollar bill that we give to God and that's the end of it, we give our one hundred dollar bill to God and he accepts it but says, "This is mine, but I want you to cash it in for pennies and give one penny back to me each day." It's a daily death.

What's it look like to die every day? Well, dying to yourself today may mean spending your lunch hour sitting with someone who doesn't have anyone to sit with. It may mean grabbing some friends and serving at a homeless shelter downtown. Dying to yourself may mean changing your spring break plans and going on a mission trip instead. Dying to yourself may mean using your lawn mowing or babysitting money to sponsor a child who won't get a meal today. Dying to yourself may mean going ahead and forgiving the person who doesn't deserve it and hasn't even asked for it. Dying to yourself may mean that you selflessly love. Why don't you push pause for a minute and write down in the space some of the ways that you can carry a cross and die to yourself today?

Really, it's only by dying daily that we are even able to follow Jesus. There are many people who get frustrated in their efforts to follow Jesus. They're trying as hard as they can and don't understand why they have such a hard time, or why they're so inconsistent. One person sent me an email that read, *"Thanks so much for this challenge to go from fan to follower. I am trying everyday to become a follower of Jesus."* I appreciated that, but I can tell you he is going to fail because "trying every day" isn't enough. If I could just change one world in that email it would make all the difference. It needs to read *"Thanks so much for this challenge to go from fan to follower. I am dying every day to become a follower of Jesus."*

In my closet where I get on my knees each morning and surrender to Jesus I have three words spray-painted on the wall. They are Paul's words found in 1 Corinthians 15:31. Paul says:

I die daily.

That's the hardest part of carrying your cross… it's so daily. Each morning by the grace of Jesus, I am invited to take up a cross and die. That's the only way I will follow him that day. Every morning we crawl back on the altar and die to ourselves. That's Jesus' invitation in Luke 9:23, but look at what he says in the very next verse:

> *For whoever wants to save his life will lose it, but whoever loses his life for me will save it.*

It's only by dying to ourselves that we truly find life. When we finally let go of our lives we find real life in Christ. Those of you who have experienced this understand what Jesus is saying. For some of the fans, none of this makes sense. In fact, in 1 Corinthians 1:18 Paul wrote . . .

> *For the message of the cross is foolishness to those who are perishing, but to us who are being saved it is the power of God.*

One version puts it this way, "The message of the cross doesn't make sense..." (CEV). Dying to yourself doesn't make sense for the fan, but the follower understands that dying is the secret of really living. That's why we sing about the wonderful cross.

> The cross that represented defeat—for a follower it is an image of victory.
>
> The cross that represented guilt—for a follower it is an image of grace.
>
> The cross that represented condemnation—for a follower it is an image of freedom.
>
> The cross that represented pain and suffering—for a follower it is an image of healing and hope.
>
> The cross that represented death—for a follower it is an image of life.
>
> The cross may not be attractive, but for a follower it is beautiful.

Taking up a cross and dying to myself sounds like torture. We think that such a decision would make us miserable. Is that what it means to follow Jesus? We wake up every morning and commit to misery. But when we die to ourselves and completely surrender to him, there is a surprising side effect to dying; we discover true life. In a twist of irony, we find that giving up our lives gives us the life we so desperately wanted all along.

not a fan story

Denzel Macklin

I don't remember a whole lot about my life as a kid. Mostly the thing I remember was being scared. I felt about knee high to every adult in my life, looking up wide-eyed at every big person, frantically hoping for someone to recognize me. From the orphanage to every foster home, I came into a new loneliness. I had always been afraid of being left alone. I guess that is because my mom gave my sister and me up when I was three. I always felt like I kind of left her behind. My adoptive parents took me in when I was in third grade. They are generous people, but have never really known me, or even known where I was. They gave me up in a way too. I was baptized at age thirteen and hoped desperately that things would change, because I knew something had to. I quit caring what happened to me, or who I was becoming. I had been empty and lonely for a long time. Being alone had become a way of life. My best friends were movies, music, and skating. Two years ago, when I was a sophomore in high school, I was very lost. I had reached a point of loneliness that I cannot describe. I tried to fill it by smoking pot, and very regrettably lost my virginity to a girl I barely knew. I wish I could take that back. I was sure that God had abandoned me like everyone else — that is what I was used to. I was deeply depressed and suicide became a real thought for me, day after day while sitting with my TV I began to think it was the only way out of my lonely existence. Deep in my heart I longed to know someone cared enough about me to help me stop the nothingness that was swallowing me. That day I was thinking of killing myself, the suicide hotline called me to make sure I was okay ... actually, so many people called me that day. God heard me. I knew after that, I would not survive without entrusting my heart to the only one who had never abandoned me. God saw me. He saw that I was lost and scared. He sees my broken heart and my broken childhood. He is fixing me. He is helping me trust again. He is with me when I am alone, and when I am not. I am truly grateful to him for leading me to the doorstep of godly people who have shown me I do not have to be empty or lonely any longer. I am compelled to follow him, and he is the only Father who has never overlooked me. I am first God's child, more than the child of any drug addict, more than the child of any preoccupied adoptive father, more than even my Christian father figure. God is my perfect Father. I am staying focused on what is right. One of my favorite thoughts has become Deuteronomy. 31:6: " Be strong and courageous! For the Lord your God will personally go ahead of you. He will neither fail you or abandon you." You feel abandoned? Jesus doesn't do that. My name is Denzel, and I am no longer a fan.

part 3

following Jesus —
wherever.
whenever. whatever.

wherever.
what about there?

If anyone would come after me, he must deny himself and take up his cross daily and follow me (Luke 9:23).

When you read this invitation of Jesus there is a tendency to read it as being poetic. Even as we break it down word for word, the dramatic and radical nature of the invitation tends to draw an emotional response. But as you step across the line and commit to being a follower, it's important to understand and think through the personal and more practical implications.

At the end of Luke chapter nine, after Jesus offers an invitation to follow him, we are introduced to three people who initially seem eager to be followers. However, as they process how following Jesus will impact their specific situations, they begin making excuses. As they try to negotiate the terms of their commitment to Jesus, it becomes clear that they were really just fans.

We meet the first of these fans in verse 57. He approaches Jesus and his disciples:

They were walking along the road, a man said to him, "I will follow you wherever you go."

Those words certainly sound impressive. He seems to understand what Jesus was looking for. He knows the right words to say. He states his commitment to Jesus and says, "I will follow you wherever you go." Wherever. That sure sounds like a follower. No restrictions. No boundaries. No borders. Wherever. But look at verse 58:

Jesus replied, "Foxes have holes and birds of the air have nests, but the Son of Man has no place to lay his head."

Jesus turns to this man, and I'm guessing with a bit of a smile, says, "Hey, bro, I'm homeless." My guess is that this revelation was often a deal breaker for a lot of would-be followers. Jesus is making it clear up front that following him won't mean going from town to town staying at the Marriott, sleeping in and ordering room service.

The man says, "I will follow you wherever." And Jesus points to a place that will be a threat to this man's comfort and security and asks, "What about there?" We're left with the impression that this wannabe follower quickly rescinded his offer. *"Did I say 'Wherever'? That was meant to be more of a poetic expression. Figuratively speaking, I will follow you 'Wherever.'"*

It's much easier to speak about following Jesus when you are making a general statement without any specific commitments. But the most obvious and basic definition of following Jesus will mean making some significant life changes. Following Jesus literally means that you go where Jesus goes. When you think of it that way, suddenly those poetic words have some huge implications.

I grew up as a preacher's kid. My dad would often do the old school revivals at different churches and bring me along with him. Every night when he would finish preaching he would use the same invitation hymn, "I Surrender All." people would often respond by walking forward during this song and putting their trust in Jesus to be their Lord and Savior. I knew the song backwards and forwards: *"All to Jesus I surrender; humbly at his feet I bow. Worldly pleasures all forsaken; take me Jesus, take me now. I surrender all."* But one night when I was about ten years old, while this song was being sung I decided to surrender all. My heart was pounding. My hands were sweating. My stomach was in knots. I finally took a step out into the aisle and I walked forward. My dad was standing up front waiting to talk to anyone who might respond. I stood next to him down front and sang along with the church to the final words of the song, *"I surrender all. All to Thee my blessed Savior, I surrender all."*

But as I got older, I didn't. It was one thing to sing those words as a general commitment, but when surrendering became more specific, the song I was singing with my life wasn't "I Surrender All," it was "I Surrender Some." I didn't surrender my pride and I was often motivated more out of a desire to impress people than to glorify God. I didn't surrender my plans; God was welcome to come along, but I did what I wanted to do. He was welcome to the co-pilot seat, but I kept a firm grasp on the controls. I didn't surrender my selfish desires. I didn't surrender my lustful thoughts. I didn't surrender my entertainment choices; I watched what I wanted to watch and listened to what I wanted to listen to. I didn't surrender my money; God got the leftovers. I didn't surrender my time to God. Early on, I didn't surrender my marriage; my wife wouldn't say it, but I was sarcastic and selfish.* I didn't surrender all.

Like this first man we may be quick to say to Jesus, *"I will follow you wherever ..."* But let's move it from the general to the more specific. Where is the one place you find it most difficult to follow Jesus? If you said to Jesus *"Wherever,"* where do you think is the one place he would point to and say, *"What about there?"*

Wherever? What about in your own home? There is the tendency to carry a cross and follow Jesus, but before we walk in the door of our own home, we leave the cross on the front porch.

Instead of submitting, you stand up for your rights. Instead of serving, you sit around.

Instead of being patient, you are demanding. Instead of being encouraging, you are constantly critical.

Instead of being a spiritual leader, you are passive and apathetic in your own home. So what about there?

Wherever? What about at school? At around 8 a.m. during the week, you'll find many fans getting out of their cars or off the bus, saying to Jesus, *"You wait here. I'll be back to get you around three."* When they clock in to school they clock out of following.

---

* Okay, she might say that.

177

You justify greed by calling it a necessity.

You rationalize dishonesty by calling it way to raise your GPA.

You stay quiet about your faith at school and call it being tolerant.

I received an email from a college freshman who asked me to pray for him because he wanted to take seriously this challenge of following Jesus anywhere. Since he was the new recruit on the basketball team, no one knew yet that he was a Christian or went to church. He decided that he needed to start being bolder about his faith with his teammates. He decided to make a T-shirt with the words from Colossians 3:23 on it, and offered to pray before practice with whoever was willing. He let the team know that he was playing for the glory of God. After seeing his T-shirt, the senior team captain approached him about his faith, because he had been a leader on the team for four years and no one knew he was a Christian. He felt ashamed that he had been in this freshman's place four years ago and still hadn't shared Jesus with anyone of them. These two had passed the ball back and forth countless times, and sweat through long hours of practice together, but never knew the other one was a Christian. God renewed the senior's boldness, by way of a new freshman, who couldn't wait to get the word out that he played basketball for Jesus first, not just the school. A few weeks later, the senior wrote me and said it was a really embarrassing and convicting moment for him, knowing that the freshman had shared more about his faith in one season than he had in four. He called himself a follower, but he wasn't following on the court. So let me ask you, what about there?

Wherever? What about at the game? What about in the neighborhood? What about when you're hanging out with old friends? Or what about this: What if God points to a place like Burma or Thailand and says, *"What about there?"*

Anne Judson was the wife of America's first foreign missionary, Adoniram Judson. Adoniram was twenty-four when he decided to leave America and sail to Burma. Burma didn't have a single missionary and was an extremely hostile environment. He was in love with Anne, who was twenty-three at the time. Adoniram wanted to marry Anne and then move to Burma to spread the gospel. Before he married Anne, he wrote her father the following letter asking for her hand in marriage:

I have now to ask, whether you can consent to part with your daughter early next spring, to see her no more in this world; whether you can consent to her departure, and her subjection to the hardships and sufferings of missionary life; whether you can consent to her exposure to the dangers of the ocean, to the fatal influence of the southern climate of India; to every kind of want and distress; to degradation, insult, persecution, and perhaps a violent death. Can you consent to all this, for the sake of him who left his heavenly home, and died for her and for you; for the sake of perishing, immortal souls; for the sake of Zion, and the glory of God? Can you consent to all this, in hope of soon meeting your daughter in the world of glory, with the crown of righteousness?

Her father told him that it was her decision to make. As Anne thought about this decision, she wrote the following note to her friend Lydia Kimball:

I feel willing, and expect, if nothing in Providence prevents, to spend my days in this world in heathen lands. Yes, Lydia, I have about come to the determination to give up all my comforts and enjoyments here, sacrifice my affection to relatives and friends, and go where God, in his Providence, shall see fit to place me.

So in 1813 they left for Burma. They would experience one hardship after another. In 1824 Adoniram was put in prison. He was there for eighteen months. At night his feet were tied up and hoisted up into the air till only his shoulder and head rested on the ground. It was often 110 degrees and the mosquitoes would eat him alive at night. When he went to prison Anne was pregnant, but she walked two miles every day to plead that Judson be released. After a year in prison, eating rotting food, Adoniram had wasted away, with hollow eyes—dressed in rags and crippled from torture. His daughter, Maria, was born while he was in prison. Anne was as sick and thin as Adoniram. Her milk dried up. Mercifully the jailer actually let Judson out of prison each evening so he could take the baby into the village and beg for women to nurse the baby. Eventually Adoniram was released. Not long after that Anne died at thirty-seven from spotted fever. Because of Adoniram and Anne's efforts though, the entire Bible was translated into Burmese. Today there are 3,700 congregations that all trace their beginning to when Adoniram and Anne Judson said to God, "Wherever." God pointed to Burma and said, "What about there?"

This man in Luke 9 was happy to say wherever, until God said, "There." One of the reasons we don't follow Jesus *wherever* is that when he says there we take that more as a suggestion than as a command.

Jesus wants followers who will say yes to him before they even know the request. A follower of Jesus says, *"My answer is yes, now where did you want me to go?"* Jesus may point to Burma, or he may point across the street.

This week I listened to a story about a family that dates back to an ordinary day more than fifty years ago. It took place in a small town, St. Joseph, Illinois. It was a lazy Sunday afternoon at home for this family. Two men knocked on the door. One man was named Orville Hubbard. Orville used to work in the oil fields. He had minimal education, and was just a very normal, ordinary guy. The other guy was named Dick Wolf. Dick met this young family when their wives were in the hospital giving birth at the same time. They asked if they could come in because they wanted to talk to this family for a few minutes about something really important to them. There was not much else to do, and so the husband invited them in. He sat on the couch with his wife as Orville and Dick Wolf began to present the gospel. They talked to this family about what it really meant to have a relationship with Jesus Christ. The couple sat and listened. There is one small but important detail I don't want to leave out. There was a young boy playing with his trucks on the floor. He was about eight years old. Everyone thought he was just playing with his toys, but that little boy was hanging on every word. That day changed everything for that family. The next week the mom and dad, along with their young son, gave their lives to Christ and were baptized. Two ordinary men said "wherever," and Jesus pointed them to this family's house.

I think it's fair to say that I wouldn't be writing this book in 2011 if they hadn't done that in 1956. The couple that answered the door that day I call Grandma and Grandpa. That little eight-year-old boy playing on the floor with his trucks was my dad. So some day in heaven I'm going to thank Orville and Dick for being followers instead of fans. I'm sure they could've found other things to do that day. My guess is they were pretty nervous when they knocked on that door. I'm sure it was uncomfortable. But two men I've never met decided to follow Jesus *wherever* and they ended up on my grandparents' front porch.

Did I Say "Wherever"?

The way Jesus answers this fan in Luke 9 reveals some of the reasons it's difficult to tell Jesus, "Wherever." Jesus speaks of following him as a journey of risk and uncertainty. If the man decided he was going to follow Jesus, he didn't know where he would be going, or if he would even have a place to stay. He says no to following Jesus in part because he's afraid to say yes. Whenever we are afraid of what a commitment will lead to, our instinctual response is to say no. Fear always asks the question, *"What if?"* *What if I switch schools and it doesn't work out? What if choose the wrong major and I'm miserable? What if I get married and my marriage ends up like my parents'?* And this is what often concerns us about making a commitment to Christ. *What if he wants me to share my faith and I have to get up in front of people? What if he wants me to serve and he points to a homeless shelter? What if he wants me to be a missionary in a third-world country?* Psychologists tell us that the number-one way people deal with fear is avoidance. We just stay away from the people and places that cause us anxiety. The Old Testament prophet Jonah was told to go preach to the people of Nineveh, but Jonah was afraid and we read in chapter 1 verse 3 ... *Jonah ran away from the Lord.*

Another reason this man in Luke seems to say no to Jesus is because Jesus calls him to something uncomfortable. If you say to Jesus, *"I will follow you wherever,"* you can be sure that where he points will be out of your comfort zone. "Out of your Comfort Zone" could be defined this way: "The places where saying yes to God means saying no to me." I sent out an email to some friends and I asked them to finish this statement for me: **Saying yes to following Jesus meant saying no to ...**

Here are the responses I got:

> Saying yes to following Jesus meant saying no to living with my boyfriend.

> Saying yes to following Jesus meant saying no to hanging out at the club with the friends I've grown up with.

> Saying yes to following Jesus meant saying no to taking the job that I knew would come with too much temptation.

> Saying yes to following Jesus meant saying no to a golf scholarship so I could attend seminary.

> Saying yes to following Jesus meant saying no to my family, who doesn't believe the Bible is true.

> Saying yes to following Jesus meant saying no to the invitation to go to the party.

As I read through the responses I realized that in one way or the other everyone was really saying the same thing: *"Saying yes to following Jesus meant saying no to comfort."*

It's not only us, but it's often our families that are pushing us to lead comfortable and safe lives. They may want you to follow Jesus, but they have a hard time accepting that Jesus might lead you to a place that requires risk and sacrifice. When I was twenty-one years old I knew God was calling me to go plant a new church. But I'll never forget a conversation I had with my grandmother when I told her that we believed God was calling us to plant a new church in Los Angeles. You need to know that she is a committed Christian lady, but I think it's fair to say that she thought we were crazy. She had all kinds of questions for me. She asked, *"What if you get out there and no one comes to the church? What if you can't find any place to meet? What if the church doesn't have enough money to pay you and you can't take care of your family? Are you sure you're ready for this? What if it doesn't work out?"* And I know she was asking out of concern for me. She didn't want me to take any risks. My grandma means well, but if she had her way I'd move into her spare bedroom and she'd make me cinnamon rolls and bring me a glass of milk every morning. She was happy for me to follow Jesus "wherever" as long as "wherever" was someplace safe and secure.

Defining Wherever

The man stands before Jesus and says "wherever," but I'm not sure he really understands what he is committing himself to. And Jesus puts a little skin on his words, so he can see what the word "wherever" looks like. Jesus helps the man understand that "wherever" very well may involve traveling from town to town living as a homeless person on the street. I doubt that's what the man was thinking when he committed to "wherever."

It reminds me of when I sit down to talk to a young couple before performing their wedding. I'll try and give the bride and groom the unedited version of marriage. Many of them go into marriage with a romantic fairytale mindset and really have no idea what they're committing to. I'll try and paint a picture of what the vows they will speak to one another look like once they're a year into marriage. I'll tell the wife, "About a year into marriage you are going to be ready for bed and come into the family room and realize your husband has gained about fifteen pounds. He'll be sitting on the couch watching *SportsCenter* and slurping a huge bowl of cereal.* Between bites he'll take the spoon and use it to scratch an itch on his back." And then I turn to the soon-to-be-husband and say, "About this time she is going to start sounding a lot like your mom, telling you not to slurp and to eat your cereal at the counter. Then you'll look at her and she will look like your mom. She will be wearing the most modest nightgown ever made and have zit cream on her face." I want them to understand what they are signing up for. One of the things I will often do is go through the vows word for word and paint a scenario of what it means. These are more than poetic words that you recite on your wedding day. These words have implications:

For better or for worse. When he gets the promotion. When he gets fired. When she finds out she is pregnant. When she loses a baby. When you buy your first house. When you can't sell your first house and have to move into an apartment.

For richer or poorer. When you've got a little extra for a nice meal. When you've eaten nothing but ramen noodles for the last week. When

---

* You have to give him some credit if the cereal is Frosted Flakes.

you've saved enough to talk retirement. When you're overdrawn and bills are due.

In sickness and in health. When he's strong enough to carry you through the door. When he's older and needs to be pushed in a wheelchair. When she's young and energetic. When she's older and tired.

When we were first married, my wife and I went to see a couple in our church who were going through a difficult time. The husband had cancer and was being treated with an extremely aggressive combination of chemotherapy and radiation. Over the last several weeks, he had just wasted away. We were in his bedroom, reading Scripture and getting ready to pray for him, when we noticed a strong smell. It was obvious he'd had an accident, so I quickly prayed and we excused ourselves. I stood in the waiting room holding hands with my wife. I realized what was happening on the other side of the door. This man was too sick to control his bowels and too weak to clean himself up. His wife was changing his diaper. After a few minutes she came out and I'll never forget what she said. With a slight smile on her face she said, "In sickness and in health." And I remember thinking, "Oh. That's what those words mean."

That's what happens to this man in Luke 9. He says to Jesus, *I will follow you wherever.* Jesus says, *I have no place to lay my head.* The man thought, "Oh. That's what that word means."

Contrast this man's response in Luke 9 with what we saw when Matthew decided to follow Jesus. Matthew, as a Levite, knew that following Jesus meant leaving everything behind. He knew he was walking away from a comfortable and predictable existence to follow Jesus down an uncertain path.

When a Talmid was finally accepted as a follower of a rabbi, they would leave their homes, their jobs, and whatever else might hold them back and they would follow the rabbi, literally wherever he went. "Wherever" was not just a word used to express a commitment; "Wherever" was a way of life. So if the rabbi decided to go to market, his students would follow. And if a rabbi decided to go to another town, his students would follow. If the rabbi needed to visit someone sick in the area, his students would follow. When the rabbi slept, his students would sleep. When the rabbi ate, his students would eat. They were with him every step of every day. This idea of following the rabbi closely is captured in a Jewish saying that has become popular in Christian circles: *"May you be covered in his dust."*

The most literal way to define a "Follower of Jesus" is "Someone who goes where Jesus goes." I'm not sure how you can call yourself a follower of Jesus if you refuse to go where Jesus went. If you are following Jesus "wherever," he will take you towards a sinner that others wouldn't want to be seen with. You will find yourself among the sick that others tried to avoid. If you follow Jesus, expect to find yourself being criticized by some of the religious people in your life. If you follow Jesus you may find that your family thinks you're crazy ... his did. You may one day find yourself being unfairly accused and unjustly treated by those in political office. Ultimately if you follow Jesus "wherever," you won't just end up covered in his dust, you will end up covered in his blood.

not a fan story

Rachelle Starr

As a girl raised in a Christian home, I had never been inside a strip club in my life. But I felt this calling from God to reach out to women in the sex industry. I didn't really know how I was going to do this, but I knew that God had given me a passion for these women to know how much he loves them and how precious they are in his eyes. Still, I was definitely nervous to share the idea with others. I mean, going to a strip club isn't exactly typical for a church-raised girl. But whatever my doubts, I knew God was calling me to take action. He wanted more out of me than just having feelings of compassion for women in the sex industry. He wanted me to do something about it.

I was in my early twenties in 2008 when I started a ministry called Scarlet Hope, which reaches out to women involved in the sex industry. We take big, southern-comfort-style dinners to strip clubs. Our prayer is that we're not just feeding their stomachs, but we're feeding a deeper spiritual hunger. In some clubs, we fix hair and makeup so we can get some one-on-one time with the girls. It gives us the opportunity to pray with women in the middle of a strip club. How often does that happen?

Through this ministry, I've seen hearts changed and lives touched as many of these ladies have turned to Christ for forgiveness and a new beginning. Honestly, my heart and relationship with Jesus have also been drastically changed. I have seen Jesus show up many times in the back of a strip club dressing room. Many dancers have opened up to us, sharing their struggles, asking for prayers, and some have even accepted our invitations to church.

It's funny, but the dancers have taken to calling us "the church ladies." I never thought I'd end up with such a traditional title doing radical work for God, but I think that's the kind of church lady God was calling me to become. My name is Rachelle Starr, and I am not a fan.

whenever.
what about now?

I came across a website recently called *Mother of All Excuses*. It was set up so people could share excuses that they've used and others could take advantage of. There are over four hundred excuses to use on the job. More than five hundred excuses for cutting class are listed. There are several hundred excuses for breaking dates. There are excuses for cheating on a diet, and of course excuses for when you've been pulled over.

Here are some of my favorites that are supposedly true:

> I was late to school today because my mom forgot to get the Sunday paper off the porch yesterday, and didn't realize it was Monday when I got it this morning.

> My daughter cannot make it to school today as it is the national "take your child to work day." I don't have a job so she stayed home and helped me do the chores.

> Please excuse my daughter from turning in her homework today. Her younger brother stole it, filled in the answers, and handed it in to his teacher to prove how smart he was.

> I have to cancel my speaking engagement tonight because I punctured my eardrum by being too aggressive with my Q-tip. (Yep, that one's mine.)

The first wannabe follower we looked at in the last chapter comes *to* Jesus. But this man has Jesus come to him. We don't know much about him other than the excuse he gave for not following Jesus.

He said to another man, "Follow me." But the man replied, "Lord, first let me go and bury my father." Jesus said to him, "Let the dead bury their own dead, but you go and proclaim the kingdom of God" (Luke 9:59–60).

This man is invited by Jesus to follow him. We are not told his name. Had he agreed to follow Jesus, we would know him by name. Instead of speaking of the twelve disciples we would likely speak of the thirteen disciples. But he didn't say yes and Scripture doesn't tell us who he was and history has long since forgotten.

Jesus spoke the same two words that he spoke to Matthew and the other disciples. He offers this man this same two-word invitation that has been offered to you and me: *"Follow me."*

This man seems willing. It appears that he wants to accept the invitation to follow. The first word out of his mouth is "Lord." He refers to him with the same title a slave would give to his master. That's an indication that he knows what Jesus is asking of him. But the second word out of his mouth is the word "first." He wants to follow Jesus, but now isn't a good time. He tries to offer an excuse that can put Jesus off for a little while.

Jesus doesn't seem to be interested in this man's excuse, but I have to tell you, his excuse seems reasonable to me. He wants to have a funeral for his father. Isn't Jesus being a little too hardcore? Let the guy go bury his dad. It should be pointed out that the guy's dad was likely still living, and other than a head cold or perhaps a bum knee, was probably in good health. When the man says, *"Let me go and bury my father,"* it's another way of saying, *"When my parents die, I will follow you."* We're not sure why he was waiting for them to die.

Would they not approve of their son following this unconventional and controversial rabbi?

Was he afraid of telling them he wouldn't be carrying on the family business?

Was he waiting to receive his share of a significant inheritance?

Whatever the reason, there is a sense in which most of us resonate with his excuse. It's not that he isn't willing; it's just not good timing. He isn't saying "No"; he's saying "Not right now." I suspect there are a lot of fans who feel okay about a half-hearted relationship with Jesus, because they have every intention of one day going all-in and being completely committed. They don't feel convicted about not following Jesus because in their minds they know that one day they will. They let themselves off the hook for a lukewarm faith because they didn't tell Jesus no; they're just waiting till later.

So how does Jesus respond to this man's excuse to first go and bury his father? Jesus did not say, "I understand. You'll know when the time is right." He did not say, "I don't want to put any pressure on you. Take your time." He did not say, "Whenever you're ready I'll be waiting right here." What he said was, *"Let the dead bury their own dead."* That gives some indication of how Jesus feels about our excuses and procrastination.

Contrast this man's response to the response of the first disciples that Jesus called to follow him:

> As Jesus was walking beside the Sea of Galilee, he saw two brothers, Simon called Peter and his brother Andrew. They were casting a net into the lake, for they were fishermen. "Come, follow me," Jesus said, "and I will make you fishers of men." At once they left their nets and followed him.
>
> Going on from there, he saw two other brothers, James son of Zebedee and his brother John. They were in a boat with their father Zebedee, preparing their nets. Jesus called them, and immediately they left the boat and their father and followed him.
>
> Matthew 4:18–20

It says in verse 20, "At once" and in verse 22, it says "immediately." That's the commitment that Jesus was looking for in his followers. When fans are asked about when they will get serious about their commitment to follow Jesus, the most common answer is tomorrow. There is a tendency to treat our relationship with Jesus like the diet we keep meaning to start. *I'm going to start eating right, as soon as I finish off this chicken chimichanga. Tomorrow for sure.* We treat our relationship with Jesus like the workout program we keep meaning to start. We go to bed telling ourselves, *"Tomorrow I'm going to wake up early and exercise."* But the following night we find ourselves getting into bed promising, *"Tomorrow for sure."*

On the invitation Jesus gives us to follow him there is an RSVP date and it reads: TODAY. The word tomorrow is not in the Holy Spirit's vocabulary. When Jesus calls us to follow, he means right now. He means today.

The question is, how long have you been saying tomorrow? Technically, if you said it yesterday, then today is tomorrow and that means the time is now. But even as you read this and agree with it, there is probably part of you like this man in Luke 9 that says, "First let me ..."

I have a friend named Scott who is about ten years older than me. He told me about going to church in high school and really feeling God calling him to get serious about a relationship with him, but Scott said, *"I will, but first let me graduate from high school. I'll get serious in college."* Scott graduated from high school, and once he was in college God was once again calling him to be a committed follower and again Scott said, *"Absolutely I will, but first let me graduate from college."* After he got his diploma God said, *"What about now?"* And Scott said, *"I will, but first let me find a job."* He found a job and became consumed with his work. But he promised God, *"I'm going to get serious about following you, but first I'm going to get married and let things slow down."* Eventually he and his wife got married and had a few kids. When the kids were young he and his wife talked about getting back in church, but it never seemed like the right time. For more than twenty-five years Scott told Jesus *tomorrow.* The good news is that Scott recently heard Jesus say, "What about now?" and he responded. He finally became a completely committed follower of Christ.

His story is one I hear often. People put off following Jesus with their whole heart. For years they tell Jesus, "Tomorrow." While I'm glad tomorrow eventually came for Scott, he would tell you that he lost a lot in the land of tomorrow. His wife left him and took the kids. He gets to see them every other weekend, which has left him plenty of time to attend AA meetings. The land of tomorrow is where you find

lost relationships, addiction, and unmanageable debt. In the land
of tomorrow you will find haunting regrets and broken promises.
Tomorrow eventually comes, and carries with it all the consequences
of what we put off yesterday.

Blinking Light

For the fans who are always telling Jesus tomorrow, I've discovered
that most often tomorrow only becomes today when tragedy strikes
and dreams are shattered. After years of putting him off, they finally
turn to him in desperation, ready to surrender to him their whole life. It
may be shattered and in a thousand pieces but they finally give it over
to him.

Jesus hasn't just been whispering "Follow me" to some of you. He's
been shouting, hoping to get your attention before you lose any more
in the Land of Tomorrow. I told you about the car I used to drive called
a Plymouth Breeze. I'm not sure how I ended up purchasing that car.
No one ever plans on driving a Plymouth Breeze. It's not a car people
save up for; it's a car people end up with. It seemed like something
was always wrong with that vehicle. At one point the check engine
light came on. I opened up the hood and stared at the engine but
that's about all I knew how to do. To be fair, it wasn't an easy hood
to open. Every time I would start the car, the light would be blinking.
I convinced myself that it was nothing. I didn't have any money to fix
it anyway. But I had to do something about the blinking light. Besides
being annoying, when people would ride with me they would point it
out. *Do you know your check engine light is on?* So here's what I did …
I got a piece of black electrical tape and I put it over the blinking light
on my dashboard. Problem solved. No more blinking light. A number
of months came and went and then one day on the way home from
the grocery store I had the car in drive, I was giving it gas, but it
wasn't going anywhere. It was something called a transmission. The
manufacturer of the car had designed the engine so that if something
wasn't right the light would start blinking. It is meant to get our
attention and let us know that something is wrong. You can ignore the
light and cover it with electric tape. You can pretend like everything is

okay. But the blinking light is an early warning system, and if you pay attention to it you can save yourself stress, heartbreak, and a small fortune later. So when that light comes on, it is a call to action.

There are natural consequences that come when we refuse to follow Jesus and instead go our own way. I'm not saying that God causes those things, but I am saying that he often allows these blinking lights to get our attention so we will get on the right path and follow him.

I could tell you story after story about fans who had told Jesus "tomorrow" over and over, but it was when life suddenly became overwhelming that tomorrow became today. Todd came forward when he got caught shoplifting, only thinking about lifting the iPod, Now he's not sure how he is going get this off his record. The stress is taking its toll not just on his parents, but also on his health. For the first time in his life he is afraid. For the first time in his life his prayers aren't just repetitive phrases he learned as a child … He is in need. He is desperate and he turns to God in a way that he never would have had he not been caught. It was easy enough for him to be a fan of Jesus, when shoplifting was a lazy outlet for showing off. But now for the first time in his life he's realizing he has only been a fan, and becomes a follower.

Hannah's parents were married for more than twenty years when her dad decided he wanted to be single. Because of her anger, she no longer felt welcome at church, felt like no one understood. She came to camp on a whim, broken and bitter. But for the first time, this unforgiving young lady began to see how the Bible spoke directly to her. And she decided to listen. In her bitterness, she heard the message of Jesus saying, "Be kind to one another, tenderhearted, forgiving each other, just as in Christ, God forgave you." And she became a follower.

I am standing up performing a funeral for Alice. Her car was struck by a semi and she died instantly. She was a wonderful Christian lady. She was always at church volunteering to do whatever needed to be done. And she was always praying for her husband, Bob. Bob would visit once a year on Mother's Day to appease his wife. His eyes would be closed during most of my sermon. His arms would be crossed. As I stand behind a pulpit eulogizing his wife, for the first time I sense that he is listening and God is speaking. Later that night I go to his house and he invites me in. Her Bible is out and he has been reading it. A few weeks later he walked forward down the same aisle his wife's casket had been carried—and with tears in his eyes he said, "I'm ready."

There are plenty of other stories I could tell you: a girl is diagnosed with cancer, parents get divorced, the addiction seems unbeatable, a future seems overwhelming, a relationship falls apart . . . and something happens. Suddenly having a little bit of religion isn't enough. Jesus becomes more than a guy wearing a blue sash—he becomes the only hope and they decide to follow.

Later Becomes Never

The most dangerous part of following Jesus tomorrow isn't what you will lose between now and then. That's not the worst thing that can happen. The worst thing that can happen is that tomorrow might never come. The truth is the longer you put him off, the more likely it is that following him will never happen.

Saying "tomorrow" to Jesus is like hitting snooze on your alarm in the morning. Let's say you set your alarm for six in the morning. The alarm goes off. It wakes you up, but you could sure use ten more minutes. The next morning it goes off again and again you hit the snooze. By the next week you're hitting the snooze three or four times and the alarm is going off longer and longer before it wakes you up. I have one of the demonic alarms that gets louder and louder until you turn it off. But the more you hit snooze the harder it is for you to hear it and respond the next time, and you may eventually find that you'll just sleep right through it. Jesus says to you, *"Follow me."* But you tell him, *"Ten more minutes."* The more you put him off the less likely he is to get your attention.

When I was in college I was introduced to the "as now, so then" principle of human behavior. Simply stated the "as now, so then" principle is the idea that current habits are overwhelmingly the most likely predictor of future practices. The vast majority of the time, the decision you make today will be the decision you make tomorrow. If you don't do it now there is no reason to think you will then.

Hebrews 3:15 says, "Today, if you hear his voice, do not harden your hearts."

The time is now. The day is today. Don't tell yourself, *tomorrow I'm going to surrender my secret sin.* Don't tell yourself, *tomorrow I'm going to start being generous to those in need.* Don't tell yourself, *tomorrow I'm going to walk across the street and introduce myself to the neighbor.* Don't tell yourself, *tomorrow I'm going to check into a mission trip, or sign up for a Bible study, or volunteer at the shelter.* Today is the day to start following.

I'll never forget the funeral I did for a young lady named Brittany Bevin. She was seventeen years old when she died in a car accident. The more I learned about Brittany the more her life inspired me. Her parents allowed me to read her prayer journal so I could get to know their daughter better. I turned to the most recent entry. It was written the night before she died. Here is the prayer she wrote to God:

> *You hold the only peace that can fill the deepest hole. But how do I get it? You said, "Ask and you shall receive." I am asking and I know that you will give it to me. Every week you bless me so much and teach me lesson after lesson. I know that once again you are showing me your love. I can't fathom how much you feel when one of your children suffers, but I've had a glimpse of your heartache. Please fill me with your wisdom that I won't just watch others suffer, but that I'll be able to say what they need to hear. As a new week approaches, my dangerous prayer is that you'll place broken-hearted people in my path and fill me with You so that I can let your love heal their pain.*

Brittany had recently opened up a checking account. When her dad was closing that account he found that she had only written one check. It was to Compassion International to support a child. Before I got up to speak, her father shared a few words. Here's what he said to a sanctuary filled with her friends:

On the day Brittany died it didn't matter what kind of clothes she wore. It didn't matter who her friends were. It didn't matter where she was going to college. It didn't matter what kind of car she drove or what kind of house she lived in. It didn't matter what kind of grades she made or how many goals she scored in soccer. The only thing that mattered was that she had her faith in Christ and she knew Jesus as her Lord and Savior.

He went on to challenge the students not to wait another day because they have no guarantee. He asked the students, *"If you died today, how would you be remembered?"* The students weren't the only ones who left with the conviction that there are some things that need to change today. Not tomorrow. Today.

not a fan story

Amy Turner

You never think a taxi ride is going to change your life. I was halfway through my second trip to India, sitting in a traffic jam in the center of the Red Light District. The sun that was beaming through my window was suddenly blocked by one of the workers. Her sari was tattered and torn and her arms were bruised. She started speaking to me and then pushed her baby girl through the open window of the taxi. My friend and interpreter said that she was telling me to take the baby back home with me. This woman was so desperate for a better life for her child. I am not a mother, but I can only imagine how much she loved that little girl that was in front of me and how much more she wanted for her. I will never forget that moment.

She was not the only woman that rushed the taxi on my numerous visits to a shelter in the Red Light District. This shelter was a place for the children of sex workers to come so they didn't spend their entire day in the brothel. This shelter helps provide education and a meal for these children.

I met a young boy there named Bittu. Bittu became my best friend right away. He would sit right next to me and hold my arm as I walked around day to day. He would walk with me to the taxi at the end of the day and I would watch from the window as he walked into the maze of brothels. At night, I would think about how the rest of his day went. Was he safe? Who was around him? What did he need? What was his future going to be like? He didn't attend school, because he wasn't sponsored and his mother could not afford his education. He had a bright smile and was always so happy when we would visit the shelter.

When I got back from that trip I was determined not to let life get back to normal. I knew that following Jesus meant doing something and doing it now. He was calling me to totally step out of my comfort zone. I started a nonprofit foundation called Resc\You with my friends that had shared my first India experience. We are doing everything we can to reach out in God's love to these forgotten children living in unspeakable darkness and desperation.

John 1:5 says, "The light shines in the darkness, but the darkness has not understood it." Following what Jesus calls us to do means going to places of darkness and being a light even if it's difficult and uncomfortable. I know that this is a huge issue to tackle, but when you look that kind of desperation in the face, you find out what your faith means to you. For me, it means choosing to follow Jesus and say, "Let the little children come to me." My name is Amy Turner, and I am not a fan.

whatever.
what about that?

In Luke 9 we read about one other fan who wants to be a follower. Once again it appears that this is someone who is ready to commit to following Jesus:

> Still another said, "I will follow you, Lord; but first let me go back and say goodbye to my family" (v. 61).

There are some similarities between this fan and the one who came right before him. Apparently this guy missed out on the conversation Jesus had with the man who wanted to bury his father. This fan, like the other, agrees to follow Jesus but not right at this moment. First (there's that word again) he wants to say good-bye to his family. Once again I have to say this seems like a reasonable request. C'mon Jesus, let the guy say good-bye to his mom and pops. But most likely he's asking for more than going home for a quick hug. The cultural practice of saying good-bye to your family if you were to leave the area would have meant numerous farewell parties and could've lasted a period of weeks.

Jesus almost seems annoyed that the man would make such a request.

> Jesus replied, "No one who puts his hand to the plow and looks back is fit for service in the kingdom of God."

Jesus uses an analogy of someone plowing a field, but instead of giving full attention to his work, he looks back. Jesus knows that this man's request reveals where his heart truly lies. It's not that following Jesus wasn't important to this man, but following Jesus wasn't his top priority. Unless this man is willing to leave everything behind, it just wouldn't work. This man, like so many others we've studied, wants to follow Jesus but not with everything he has. He's not willing to go all-in. There's something else that has his attention, and he keeps looking back.

I was reading about a strange baptism practice that was allowed by the church when the Knights of Templar would be baptized. When the church would baptize one of the knights, they would be baptized with their sword, but they wouldn't take their swords under water with them. Instead they would hold their swords up out of the water while the rest of them would be immersed. It was the knights' way of saying to Jesus, "You can have control of me but you can't have this. Jesus, I'm all yours, but who I am and what I do on the battlefield, how I use this sword, that's not part of the deal." And if that was still the practice today, we might not hold up a sword, but my guess is that many would hold up a wallet. Some would hold up a remote control. Others would hold up a laptop.

Many fans say to Jesus, *"I will follow. Anything and everything I have, I give to you."* But Jesus points to what you're hiding behind your back and says, *"What about that?"* For Nicodemus it was a religious reputation. For the Rich Young Ruler it was his stuff. For this man it seems to be his family relationships that held him back. They are willing to follow Jesus, but the relationship isn't exclusive. They're holding on to some things from the past.

Imagine it this way — you've been dating someone for a few months and things start to get a little more serious. You sit down to have a D.T.R. talk and the person expresses a desire to move from a casual relationship to something more committed. You make it clear that you, too, are ready to take that next step. You assume that means things are exclusive, but a few days later you borrow the person's phone and see that a number of calls have been made and received from someone they used to date. Well, that's going to be a problem. If they are going to be committed to you, that means they won't be looking back. It's not going to work if they put a hand to the plow, but are looking over their shoulder at some other romantic relationship from the past.

Jesus doesn't want followers who have a divided affection or a split allegiance. And so Jesus points to what you most value and are most concerned about, and says, *"What about that?"*

For Pam, Jesus was asking, "What about food?" For years she turned to food rather than Jesus as her source of comfort and satisfaction. She finally realized she couldn't call herself a follower of Jesus if she was unwilling to surrender this area of her life to him.

Steve said, "I want to follow Jesus with everything." And Jesus asked, "What about your entertainment choices?" Steve wanted to be a follower of Jesus, but for a long time he kept looking back to television shows and internet sites that filled him with lust. He wanted to follow Jesus, but not with both hands on the plow; he kept looking back.

Jesus says to Stephanie, "What about your friends?" Stephanie called herself a follower of Jesus, but her life didn't revolve around Jesus. Her life revolved around her friends. Her friends were where she found her greatest joy. Her friends determined whether it was a good day or a bad day.

To Doug, Jesus asks, "What about your money?" Over the years Doug had found his identify and self-worth not in being a follower of Jesus, but in money and the things money could buy. With a downturn in the economy Doug has begun to realize that though he said he would follow Jesus, he has spent most of his time and given most of his attention to looking back.

There's a great story in the Old Testament that illustrates the kind of commitment Jesus is looking for. We read about it in 1 Kings 19. The prophet Elijah was told to select Elisha as his successor. When he finds him, Elisha is in a field plowing with twelve yoke of oxen. This is an indication of Elisha's wealth. He was doing pretty well for himself. As Elijah approached I wonder if he thought, "This might not be an easy sale; Elisha will be leaving a lot behind." If Elisha was going to respond to God's invitation to follow him as a prophet, it would require leaving behind his friends, his family, and his successful career. When Elisha heard the invitation, he didn't try and keep his business going on the side. He didn't try and negotiate the contract so it could be more of a part-time deal. Instead we read that Elisha slaughtered his twenty-four oxen. He then got together all of his farm plows and lit them on fire. The people of the community came to his farm and he barbequed the oxen and served it up to all his neighbors. He was making a clear statement that he would not be looking back. He wanted to give his full attention to the plow God had given him, so he burned all his old ones. He was not about to turn back.

When you accept the invitation of Jesus to follow him, you are not just saying that he is a top priority in your life; you are making him the only priority in your life. He desperately wants you, but he won't share you. He will settle for nothing less than your undivided attention and complete commitment. He wants you to invest in him more than your car or your clothes. He wants you to surrender to him more of your time than your friends get from of you. He wants you to expel more joy and energy in worshiping him than you do watching the big game.

When I was in high school, some close friends of my parents were going through a divorce. She had been unfaithful. The affair had been ongoing and her husband was devastated, just totally broken. But he loved his wife, and he wanted to make the marriage work. But the other man in the picture wanted her too. They were both pursuing her. They were both coming after her. She had to make a choice.

One night in the middle of all this, my dad came up to my room to pray with me, and we prayed about this family. But before we prayed, we talked a little about the situation. I said to my dad, "What would you do if something like this happened to you? What would you do if you were the husband?"

I'll never forget his response. It wasn't what I was expecting. My dad is one of the most gentle and grace-filled men you'll ever meet. But he said to me, "Well, I'd go downstairs. I'd get your wooden baseball bat. I'd drill a hole through the handle. I'd tie a leather strap to that bat. I'd put that strap around my wrist. I'd go over to the man's house and tell him that if he got within one hundred yards of my wife, I would break both his legs."

Then he's like, "Let's pray." And I just remember being a little surprised at the response. As a high school kid, I didn't get it. As a married man, I understand.

This is how God loves us, and how he wants to be loved by us. Please understand: Jesus loves you so much. He died to have a relationship with you. He will not share your heart with anyone. He will settle for nothing less than your complete devotion and heartfelt affection. He made no compromises when he came and gave his life up for you, and he takes no compromises now as he asks you to do the same.

The reason Jesus is so adamant about followers surrendering everything is because the reality is this: the one thing we are most reluctant to give up is the one thing that has the most potential to become a substitute for him. Really what we're talking about here is idolatry. When we are to be following Jesus, who is ahead of us, but find ourselves looking behind us, we are revealing that we are substituting something or someone for him.

When we finally surrender that one thing, we discover the satisfaction that comes from following Jesus that was always missing when we were holding something back.

I know there is a reluctance to go all-in and give Jesus anything and everything. We're afraid of what we'll lose. But Jesus says, *"Do you love me? Do you trust me? Then surrender everything and come follow me."* Trading everything we have for all that he offers is the best deal we could ever make. Jim Elliot, the famous missionary who gave his life trying to reach the Auca Indians of Ecuador, once put it this way: *"He is no fool who gives what he cannot keep to gain that which he cannot lose."*

Psalm 106:19–20 reflects back on the Israelites worshiping a golden image while Moses was on the mountain receiving the Ten Commandments from God. Here's how the psalmist explains what they did:

They made a calf at Mount Sinai; they bowed before an image made of gold. They traded their glorious God for a statue of a grass-eating bull (NLT).

That's just not a good trade. But when we hold something back, we are exchanging that which we refuse to surrender for the opportunity to follow Jesus.

Have you exchanged obediently following Jesus for a car that can really handle the corners? Have you exchanged following Jesus for a party scene that is making you life exciting? Have you exchanged following Jesus for being more popular at school? Have you exchanged following Jesus for following your fantasy football league? That's just not a good trade. Understand it's not that any of those things are wrong or sinful in and of themselves, but for too many of us these good things become God things. They have become too important and they keep us from following Christ with our whole hearts. Augustine referred to these things as "disordered loves." They may very well be legitimate, but they are out of order in our lives.

As a pastor I have performed dozens and dozens of funerals over the years. More often than not, the person who has passed away is not someone I knew. In order to help me speak about the deceased on a more personal level, I invite the family to gather around and share stories and memories of their loved one. They tell me about the person's hobbies and what they were passionate about. These are the ways the person is known and identified. He was an avid golfer. She was a prolific quilt maker. He was a huge sports fan. She was a gifted decorator. He loved a good cigar and was a passionate cigar collector. She loved Broadway shows and was a huge fan of *The Phantom of the Opera*. He was a car enthusiast. She was a talented musician. He was a brilliant businessman. She was the most loving mother. He was the most encouraging dad.

I write down the different ways they describe the person who has passed away. But the whole time the person is being remembered and described, I'm praying, "Please tell me the person loved Jesus. It's great she's an affectionate mom and gifted decorator and a talented musician, but please say she was a follower of Jesus."

Ultimately that's all that matters. It appears that this guy in Luke 9 didn't become a follower of Jesus because he put his family ahead of following Christ. And maybe when he passed away someone stood up and said about him, "He was a family man. Nothing mattered more to him than family. He always put his family first." And maybe those who were sitting there thought to themselves, "What a wonderful way to be remembered, he put his family first." But we know that on one day in this man's life he came face to face with the Son of God. And he had the opportunity to become his follower and be a part of changing the world forever. The fact that he put his family first isn't a testament to his character, but evidence of his foolishness. He put his family ahead of following Jesus. In the end that isn't a good trade.

What is it that is competing for your allegiance to Christ? You may have both hands on the plow, but what is it you keep looking back at? Until you really have surrendered anything and everything over to Jesus and truly put him above all else in your life, you will not know the joy and satisfaction that finally comes when you go all-in.

When I was in high school, I read the biography of William Borden. His commitment to following Christ had a significant impact on my decision to serve the Lord in ministry. William Borden will forever be known as "a follower of Christ." There are plenty of other ways he could have been described. He could have been described as a "multimillionaire." He was born in the late 1800s. He was the heir of a family fortune, a dairy company that is worth billions today. He could be described as an "Ivy-league graduate." He did his undergraduate work at Yale and earned a graduate degree from Princeton. But William Borden decided to be known as a follower of Christ. He left his millions and followed the call of Jesus to an unreached Muslim people group.

After he had graduated from high school his parents sent him on a tour around the world. As he traveled across Europe, Asia, and the Middle East, God began to call him to reach out to the lost people who had never heard the Good News of the gospel. He wrote home to tell his parents he was giving his life to Jesus on the mission field. On that trip he wrote two words in his Bible:

No Reserves.

He knew that following Jesus in this way would require a complete commitment. William's father insisted that he attend the university so he enrolled at Yale. His freshman year, he found that his passion for Christ was not shared by many, so he began meeting with a friend in the morning to read the Bible and pray together. Before long other students joined them and it became a revival on that campus as students met in different groups for Bible study and prayer. By the time William was a senior, one thousand of the students were a part of one of these groups. One entry he recorded in his personal journal during that time simply said, "Say no to self and yes to Jesus every time."

During his time at Yale, Borden also worked with the homeless and the hurting who were living on the streets of New Haven. He founded and personally funded the Yale Hope Mission in an effort to rehabilitate alcoholics and addicts. His father died while he was at Yale, leaving William with a significant family fortune. Upon graduation from Yale, Borden wrote two more words in the back of his Bible:

No Retreats.

He knew that following Jesus meant that he couldn't look back. He knew Jesus was calling him to world missions and decided to take the gospel to the Kansu people in China. Before going to China, he went to Egypt where he could learn the Arabic language and prepare for his ministry to Muslims. While he was in Egypt he caught spinal meningitis. William Borden died one month later at the age of twenty-five. He was buried in Cairo.

There might be some who would say that he didn't make a good trade. He gave up his family, his fortune, and a future career to follow Jesus as a missionary and he died before he reached the mission field. But this man, who sparked a revival at Yale and ministered to hundreds through his Mission, and has inspired thousands of missionaries with his commitment, knew he had made the right decision. After his death there were three phrases found written inside the Bible of this completely committed follower of Jesus:

No Reserves.

No Retreats.

No Regrets.

Is that the way you are living your life as a follower of Christ? What would change if you were to go all-in and be completely committed in following Jesus?

I want you to imagine that when your life is over, that instead of being taken directly to heaven you find yourself sitting alone in a giant movie theater. This isn't exactly how you thought it was going to happen, and it would be nice if popcorn were provided, but you wait patiently for the show to start. The lights are dimmed and the opening credits of the movie begin to roll. Immediately you realize that you know most of the cast. Your parents, your spouse, your children, your friends are all in the movie. But your name receives the top billing. Apparently you're the star of this film. The title flashes up on the screen: "Fan or Follower —A What-If Story."

The opening scene of the movie begins to unfold. Initially you recognize the scene as a real-life event, but then it takes a much different direction than what happened in reality. Theologians actually debate this whole idea of whether or not God, who is all knowing, knows the future but also knows all possible futures. But here each scene in the movie begins with something that really happened but has an ending that isn't consistent with what really happened in your life.

The first scene comes on and it's immediately familiar to you. You're sitting at a table on a first date. As you listen to the dialogue of the movie, you remember the conversation. It becomes clear that the person you are on a date with isn't a Christian, but you had a lot of fun and decide to continue the relationship. As you watch it you realize this is when you started to turn away from God. It was the beginning of a long season of spiritual dryness. But in this movie, things go differently. You invited the person to church, but your date has no interest. You decided there is no relationship there. Words come up at the bottom of the screen that read: TWO MONTHS LATER. You are in a church service when that same date comes in and sits next to you and says, *"I thought I would give this a try."*

The next scene you remember well. You are sitting in a travel agency with your spouse, flipping through pamphlets of what kind of cruise you're going to take. And you remember what happened; you chose a beautiful Caribbean Cruise and it was awesome. But in the movie things take a different turn. You set down the pamphlet and remember the mission trip that the church was going to be taking around the same time. You ask your spouse if you can talk outside for a minute. You share your crazy idea. On the way home you call the church and you say, "You know, my spouse and I have been talking and we'd like to go on a mission trip this year with our vacation time." You watch as the movie shows the two of you visiting an orphanage in Guatemala. The two of you serve food to the children and you watch as you and your spouse sit on either side of a young girl for lunch. There is a jump cut in the movie, and in this scene the two of you are sitting on either side of that little girl, but as the shot widens you realize you're in your home around your own dinner table.

The scenes continue. You see yourself on the job. A person comes by your office. The scene seems vaguely familiar to you. You recognize this person but you can't quite place their name. However, you do remember they were one of those high-maintenance people and you had established some boundaries early on so you wouldn't constantly have to hear their problems. But in this movie things go differently. You sit down with them and you listen to them. Then you say, *"Can I pray for you?"*

The scene changes. You know this one very well. You and your spouse are watching the news. You always did this. It was a nightly ritual. A little news followed by a late-night talk show. But in this movie things go differently. You turn the TV off and you watch as the two of you get on your knees beside the bed. You interlock fingers and you begin to pray. As you watch this movie you notice that it's not just the scenes that are different in your alternative life as a follower. You are different. There is a joy and a soul satisfaction that comes when we follow Jesus with our whole hearts, and it can't be found anywhere else.

What are the scenes that would unfold differently in your life if you were a follower instead of a fan? A job, marriage, and family may seem a long way off, but how much differently would your life look in the future if you started to follow Jesus completely right now? No excuses. Wherever. Whenever. Whatever.

I've discovered that the most common reason people give for not following Jesus is they want to get their lives together first. It sounds noble, like you are taking the invitation of Jesus so seriously you want to wait to start following him until you get your life turned around and going in the right direction. But when Jesus invites you to follow him, his invitation comes to you right where you are. He doesn't want you to wait until tomorrow in hopes that you will finally be heading down the right path; he wants you to say yes today and he will lead you out of where you are now.

I have a GPS on my phone, but I rarely use it. I tend to think I know where I'm going, even when I don't. For the most part, every time I use the GPS, I've tried finding something myself but have managed to get lost. When I do type my destination into my phone, the first question that comes on the screen is this: "Directions from current location?" In other words, "Do you want to start where you are?" And then it begins calculating my route, not from where I started, or the direction I should be headed, but from where I am currently located. When Jesus invites you to follow he wants you to start right now from your current location. You don't have to go back to where you started. You don't need to get a little closer on your own. He reaches out to you with grace and love and invites you to follow him. He wants you to start following him from right where you are and he wants you to start right now.

> For the eyes of the LORD range throughout the earth to strengthen those whose hearts are fully committed to him.
>
> 2 Chronicles 16:9

acknowledgments

Following Jesus is a journey that God didn't intend for us to make alone. Many of the same people I travel with down this road called "following" are the same people I want to thank for helping with this book:

To my wife, DesiRae—Thank you for your constant encouragement and support as I wrote this book about following Jesus. Thank you for your patience and grace when it doesn't describe my life. It's hard to imagine following Jesus without you by my side.

To my sister Karissa—Thanks for your work in making this teen edition come together.

To Taylor Walling, Luke Davidson, and Heath Williams—Thank you for your research, editing, and insights.

To the students of Southeast Christian Church and to my "Not a Fan" Facebook friends—It's great to be following Jesus with a community of more than 50,000 people from sixteen different countries. Hearing your stories inspired me to write this book and showed me what it looks like to follow Jesus.

notes

1. Andre Agassi, *Open: An Autobiography* (New York: Knopf, 2009).

2. Daniel Murphy, "Vows of Cohabitation," *The Door*, January/February, 2000, 21.

3. www.msnbc.msn.com/ID/4541605/NS/health-fitness

[it's a movement]

[it's a sermon series]

[it's a small group DVD series]

[it's a revival]

In order to follow, you must keep moving. Continue the journey from fan to follower. Visit **notafan.com or call toll-free (877) 578-8346** for additional resources and information.

Not A Fan Resources include:

- Small Group DVD studies
- Pastor's Resource Kit
- Feature Movie

- T-shirts
- Bracelets
- and more

Visit the Not A Fan website and enter the promo code below to receive an exclusive offer of 20% off your order of Not A Fan resources.

City On A Hill

PRODUCTIONS